Home Canning & Freezing

BY JACQUELINE HERITEAU

GROSSET
GOOD LIFE
BOOKS

PUBLISHERS • GROSSET & DUNLAP • NEW YORK

Acknowledgments

Cover photograph by Mort Engel
Drawings by Peter Kalberkamp

To Kate Alfriend, Office of Communications, U.S. Department of Agriculture, to the Research and Communications departments of Best Foods, Kerr Glass Manufacturing Corporation, and Ball Jar Corporation, my thanks for recipes, information on equipment, and for photographs relating to canning and freezing. To Karen Tierney, of Sharon, Connecticut, my thanks for the organic recipes. To artist Peter Kalberkamp, my thanks for turning incomprehensible squiggles into lovely art. To editor Lee Schryver, my gratitude for many hints and tips on canning and freezing as practiced by him and his wife. My gratitude to Evelyn H. Johnson, Ph.D., specialist in food and nutrition with the U.S. Department of Agriculture Extension Service in Washington, D.C., for her technical advice.

My thanks to the following organizations for their permission to use the photographs in this book: Dudley-Anderson-Yutzy, Public Relations, Inc.: p. 88, p. 89; Frigidaire Home Environment Division of General Motors: p. 60 left, p. 60 right, p. 61, p. 62, p.66 top, p. 66 bottom, p. 69, p. 71 top, p. 71 bottom, p. 78 top, p. 78 bottom left, p. 78 bottom right, p. 79, p. 85; Karo Division of Best Foods Corporation: p. 54; Kerr Glass Manufacturing Corporation: p. 34, p. 35 top left, p. 35 bottom left, p. 35 top right, p. 35 bottom right, p. 36 top left, p. 36 bottom left, p. 36 top right, p. 36 bottom right, p. 37 top, p. 37 bottom, p. 49.

Instructions for recipes and safety precautions in this book are in accord with the standards of the U.S. Department of Agriculture and have been carefully checked for accuracy. However, the author and publisher do not warrant or guarantee results and cannot be responsible for any adverse consequences resulting from the use of information contained herein. The author has attempted to assist the reader in avoiding problems by setting forth appropriate and recommended procedures.

Contents

Introduction

Are Canning and Freezing for You?

The answer to that question is *yes!* if you would like to lower your food budget while increasing the nutritional value of your meals—*and* if you love the luxury and delicious taste of the homemade. I'm not suggesting that you should put up everything in sight, but if you love asparagus (a luxury item for all but two months of the year) you can have superb asparagus on a shoestring if you buy in quantity during the season and put it up for the months when the cost of this delicacy is out of sight.

Luxury items, of course, are not the only savings. Fruits, tomatoes for juice or cooking, steaks, fillets, chops, ground beef, and herbs are only a few of the many staples that can be frozen and canned. For example, if green beans are a regular feature at your house, you can save as much as half what you normally spend during the winter by canning and freezing beans when they are plentiful, economical, and at their delicious, nutritious best.

By canning and freezing your own, you add to the value of your meals two ways: first, by increasing the variety of foods available on the budget; and, second, by capturing the high nutritional content of fruits and vegetables when they are garden fresh. The best way to have garden-fresh vegetables and fruits is to grow your own. Locally grown produce purchased from roadside stands and friendly farmers, if canned or frozen at once, come a close second.

The big bonus in doing your own canning and freezing is the flavor that says *homemade*. Vegetables, fruits, meats, stews, and pastries that you have prepared for canning and freezing with loving attention have something that mass-produced canned and frozen foods will never equal.

To the guest and to the family, "homemade" means warmth, and caring—two very special luxuries.

Part I
Getting the Goods

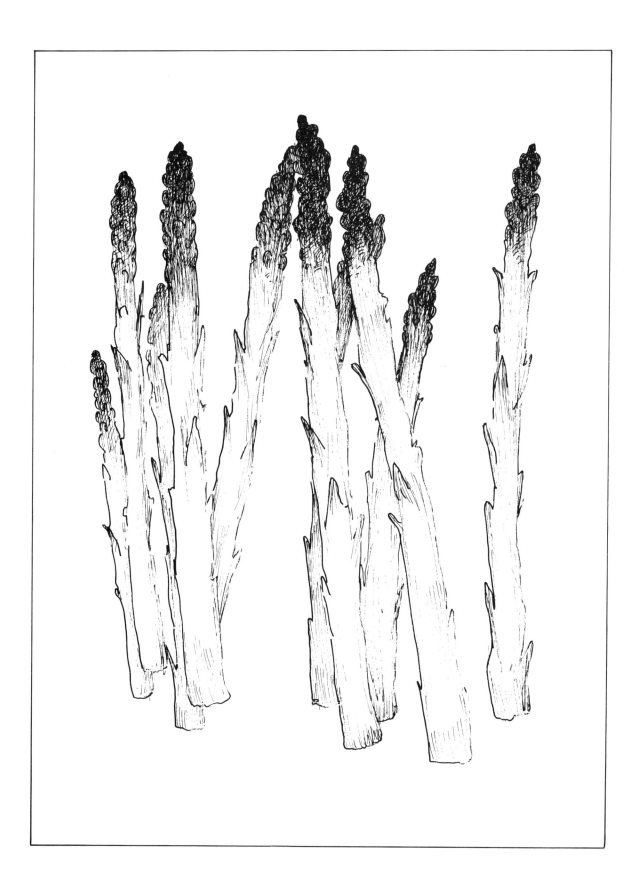

1
What to Can and What to Freeze: Method Index of Recipes

Should you plan to can or freeze or do both? To know the answer to this you have to know your real purpose in putting up food. Are you trying to lower the food budget drastically or are you looking for luxury items at budget cost? Are you interested in saving time as well as money? Do you want more of your own homemade dishes at the dinner table?

The answer to these questions and a glance at the next few pages will suggest a canning and freezing plan and leave you feeling it is all very worthwhile.

If your prime concern is to poke a hole in a ballooning food budget, then you should consider both canning and freezing. Freezing is faster and easier, but not everyone has a freezer large enough to store everything that can be put up profitably. Also, frozen foods should be used up within three to twelve months, while canned foods can sit on dusty shelves in the basement for at least two years without losing their flavor.

If you live in a city apartment without a basement or freezer, you can still find it profitable to can and freeze in batches small enough to suit your storage space. When storage space is a problem, it is most rewarding to deal only with high-priced luxury items, such as asparagus, spring peas, berries, steaks, fillets, and chops.

If you are interested in saving time as well as money, use your energies to put up precooked items mainly for the freezer. Stews, pies, sauces, stocks, breads, and pastries can be cooked in extra-large quantities and frozen. Canning will save time, too: Canned fruit compotes are delicious, as are stocks for gourmet cooking and nutritious soups.

The truth is, you can can almost anything you can freeze and you can freeze almost anything you can can. However, there is a "best way" to put up each item in this book, the way that gives the optimum in flavor, and the index below in this chapter indicates which is which. Recipes for each method are listed, the preferred way first.

The Three Ways to Can

When I talk about canning, I am really describing three possible methods of putting up food in glass jars. (You can use tin cans, but the equipment is expensive. Until you've thoroughly investigated your own pleasure and satisfaction in canning, it is a good idea to use glass jars and the simpler methods described below.)

The three ways in which foods are processed for home canning are by pressure canner, by boiling water bath (*water-bath canning*), and by the *open-kettle* method. "Processed" means made safe for long-term storage.

The pressure canner method processes prepared, raw, or partially cooked ingredients in jars that are sealed and steamed in a pressure canner at 240°F. This method is used for foods low in acid content and is the only method that destroys the bacteria that cause spoilage in low-acid foods. (See Chapter 4.)

The boiling water-bath method processes prepared, but not precooked, foods in jars that are sealed and boiled in a large kettle at 212°F. This method is used for foods that have a distinctly acid content, tomatoes for instance. Since almost everyone has a large kettle, it's a good method for a first attempt at canning, since it doesn't require the purchase of a pressure canner. However, only certain foods can safely be stored after canning by the water-bath method. (See Chapter 5.)

The open-kettle method is used to process jams, jellies, preserves, and pickles. The foods are first cooked in a big open kettle, then packed and sealed in sterilized jars, and processed in a boiling water bath. This method is suitable (and safe) only for preserves cooked with sugar or vinegar. If you decide to can jams, jellies, pickles, or preserves, *do* process them even if your recipes don't insist on processing.

Five Ways to Freeze Foods

There are five ways foods to be frozen are handled: (1) Some require only buying and wrapping; (2) others must be *blanched* in boiling water for a few minutes before they are packaged and frozen; (3) others are sprinkled with sugar; (4) others are packed in syrup before freezing; and finally, (5) the texture of carrots, whole or sliced, is disappointing when frozen, whereas pumpkin is used mashed, whether for pies or as a vegetable, so what happens to its texture doesn't matter.

What it comes down to is, the table below reflects my prejudices and you don't have to abide by them. If you love frozen carrots, then select young carrots, peel them, blanch them for five minutes in water to which you have added a tablespoon each lemon juice and brown sugar, cool, pack, and freeze them as described in Chapter 8. If I have omitted from the canning or freezing list some other vegetable that appeals to you, search the list for a vegetable that has similar consistency and texture and follow the instructions for putting up the one omitted.

The suggested method is listed to help you decide if you have the required storage space, the equipment needed, and the desire to get involved with that technique before you buy in quantity any of the foods listed.

Method Index of Recipes

Recipe	Page	Method
Apple rings: spiced	50	water-bath canner
Apple slices	80	frozen
Applesauce	50	water-bath canner
Apricots: whole	50	water-bath canner
Apricots: sliced	80	frozen

Recipe	Page	Method
Artichokes	71	frozen
Asparagus	72	frozen
	40	pressure canner
Beans: lima	72	frozen
	40	pressure canner
Beans: green; snap; wax	72	frozen
	40	pressure canner
Beef stock	40	pressure canner
Beets	41	pressure canner
Berries	80	frozen
	51	water-bath canner
Biscuits	83	frozen
Blackberries	80	frozen
Blanquette de veau	88	frozen
Blueberries	80	frozen
Bouquet garni	85	frozen
Brandied cheese spread	86	frozen
Broccoli	72	frozen
Brown-and-serve rolls	84	frozen
Brussels sprouts	72	frozen
Butter	68	frozen
Cakes	84	frozen
Capri butter	55	water-bath canner
Carrots	41	pressure canner
Cauliflower	41	pressure canner
	72	frozen
Celery and tomatoes	42	pressure canner
Chard	72	frozen
Cheese puffs	86	frozen
Cheese: soft and semi-soft	68	frozen
Cherries	51	water-bath canner
Cherries: sour	80	frozen
Cherries: sweet	80	frozen
Collard greens	73	frozen
Cookies	84	frozen
Corn: whole kernel	42	pressure canner
	73	frozen
Corn: cream style	43	pressure canner
Cranberries: whole	81	frozen
Cranberries: sauce	51	water-bath canner
Cream	68	frozen
Doughnuts	84	frozen
Eggs	67	frozen
Fish	67	frozen
Fruit and nut breads	83	frozen
Green onions	73	frozen
Herbs	73	frozen

2
How to Make Canning and Freezing Pay Off

Canning and freezing create dollar-and-cents savings when you put up bargain buys in fruit, vegetables, and meats, when the produce is really fresh and in prime condition, and when it is processed within hours of buying. This means that you should have available the basic equipment and supplies needed for canning and freezing so that when you run across a real buy in cost and freshness, you can rush home with your prize and process it at once.

The quality of your homemade foods will be only as good as the quality of the raw materials you select. Everything you use should be in perfect condition and at the peak of its flavor and texture. If you are growing your own fruits and vegetables, plant the varieties listed by the catalogs as especially suited for canning or freezing. If the fruit and vegetables come from the roadside stand or the supermarket, be highly selective about quality.

The importance of freshness, particularly in vegetables, can't be overstressed. If foods are allowed to stand several days or even hours between the time of harvesting and the time of processing, changes take place within the foods that lessen their flavor, their nutritional value, and their keeping ability.

Selecting Fruit for Canning and Freezing

Fruit for canning and freezing must be fully ripe—preferably vine- or bush-ripened—and firm. Fruit that is still on the greenish side will not be as sweet as fully ripened fruit and the true flavor will not yet have developed. Select boxes or bushels that contain fruit of uniform size if possible. Check to make sure the fruit at the bottom of the box is as ripe and firm as fruit at the top of the box. Every single fruit to be put up must be free of bruised spots, decay, or any kind of spoilage. You can't examine every piece of fruit in a bushel, of course, but you can look it over carefully without arousing the ire of the vendor—and you should. Don't buy a box containing more bruised fruit than you can use fresh.

Examine with particular care the small fruits, such as cherries, plums, and berries. The fruits on top of the box often look perfect, while those on the bottom may show evidence of mildew or crushing. Small fruits are delicate and apt to bruise more easily than the larger, firmer fruits.

Selecting Vegetables for Canning and Freezing

Vegetables are at their absolute flavorful best when they are picked young. Big, tough, overmature vegetables will result in canned and frozen goods that are tough and flavorless. The flavor depends both on early picking and on processing very shortly after picking. The sweetness of corn and peas changes especially rapidly after picking. If possible, arrange to pick these yourself. Some farm markets will allow consumers to do their own harvesting, often at a lower price per pound.

If you have ever grown your own, you can tell at a glance when vegetables are fresh. Here are a few rules of thumb: Crispness indicates freshness. Green beans and snap beans, peas and lima beans in the pod, cucumbers, and tomatoes look plump when really fresh, and have a sheen. Snap a bean in two. It will be brittle and break easily if it is fresh, but if it is old, it will bend before it breaks. Beans have the best flavor when they are picked 6 to 8 inches long and are pencil-slim. Fresh cucumbers, summer squash, and zucchini are shiny and plump and have a crisp skin that breaks easily under pressure from a fingernail. When tomatoes have been around for a while, they develop soft spots or acquire a faintly wrinkled look. Check tomatoes for green on the underside. They should be red all over.

Vegetables with foliage—carrots and beets and greens such as kale and spinach—are fresh when the leaves are crisp and the stems brittle. Carrots and beets are best when small. Greens are best when the leaves are young enough to have a curl to them.

Broccoli and cabbage is best when the buds are tightly curled and held closely together in the head by crisp young stems. Blanched cauliflower is prettiest when put up, so try to avoid heads that have a faint green or purple haze. The purple-headed cauliflower sometimes offered in specialty food markets turns green when cooked, so this decorative novelty loses much of its charm when cooked and won't look as appealing as the pure white cauliflower.

Pumpkins and winter squash seem to hold their flavor and texture for many weeks after harvesting, so you needn't be as fussy about when they were picked. However, don't buy either vegetable if it has soft spots or a wrinkled look.

Frozen asparagus tastes almost as fresh processed as it does when it was freshly picked. Try to buy asparagus for freezing from local growers, as opposed to imported Southern-grown produce, and buy as soon as the prices begin to come down early in the season. The first harvests of spears seem to be the most tender. For one thing, buyers are asparagus-hungry and buy up whatever is put out. As a result, the asparagus display is apt to have been delivered hours ago. Choose medium-sized spears if available, with a good green color and tightly closed tips. Blanched asparagus is rarely offered in local markets, and so rarely gets to the home freezer. Blanched asparagus is the fancy white asparagus offered in glass jars at the supermarket at a much higher price than ordinary green spears. If you do run across such a treasure at a reasonable price, freeze it as you would green asparagus. It's a gourmet item.

Selecting Meats for Freezing and Canning

Beef, lamb, pork, chicken, and turkey can be home-grown, just like vegetables. Most of us have neither the space nor the time for this enterprise, so bargains in meats depend on sales in the local markets or an "in" with a wholesaler. (More about that below.)

If you do raise your own, arrange to have a commercial establishment slaughter, chill, and butcher the animals—otherwise, you may mishandle the meat and be disappointed in the processed package. Animals can be slaughtered at any time of the year, and a commercial establishment will handle the meat under the sanitary conditions and controlled temperatures required by government regulations as a safeguard to the public.

If you are buying from local markets offering such favorites as steaks, chops, ground meat, and fillets at sale prices, look your bargains over carefully to make sure they are bargains. Meats packaged with cardboard on the bottom sometimes hide a massive bone or a lot of fat. If the sale is going to last several days, sample the quality of the meat at a dinner. Then if you are satisfied that it really is a bargain, buy in quantity. Meat must be repackaged for freezing (see Chapter 7) as soon as you get it home, and then frozen at once.

While it is true that frozen meats are sometimes tenderized by the freezing, it is not true that tough meat will be made tender by freezing. So select with care.

Buying meat is subject enough for a whole book. However, there are some generalizations that can be made. Marbled meats—meat with a network of thin, fatty lines running across the grain—are usually more tender, because these fatty veins melt when the meat is cooked. Meats without a marbled effect may be firmer. This is not true of fillet of beef, which is the tenderloin, and very tender, without being layered with fat. Avoid chops that have little tenderloins and a lot of gristle and fat at the tip. Inspect each piece before selecting it.

Ground beef is a frequent sale item and ground top or bottom round is most worthy of valuable storage space. Each butcher adds a certain quantity of fat to the ground meat when it is put through the machine. If you are planning to use the meat for hamburgers or ground beef steaks, look for consistency of red in the meat; a lot of pink is an indication of excess fat.

Roasts, chickens, and turkeys, when offered at good prices, are worth buying if you have a large freezer. These items are often frozen before they are offered, and sometimes butchers will sell them still frozen to consumers who buy in quantity. Ask if the frozen meats are available before you buy the counter items, but always repackage frozen meats when you get home.

Try to put up only good-quality meat from carcasses that have been aged about one week.

If you're lucky enough to have a hunter friend or relative, consider freezer space for their offerings, and package these as you would meat purchased from the store.

Dairy Products for Freezing

Eggs, butter, cream, milk, and cheese can be frozen, but buys in these items are rarely alluring enough to warrant giving them freezer space. If you have lots of freezer space and do run into good buys, be sure the products are super-fresh. Freeze pasteurized milk and whipped heavy cream to avoid spoilage of the excess you can't use, but don't plan to store these for economy's sake. The texture of frozen hard or semi-soft cheeses is somewhat off after thawing, but the flavor is usually good.

Fish and Shellfish for Freezing

Really fresh fish, oysters, shrimp, crab, fish roe, and lobster can be frozen successfully. They are well worth giving space to if you can find them at bargain prices. Processing is discussed on page 67. The only caution here is that they be absolutely fresh, caught only hours before processing. Fish deteriorates more rapidly than meat (hence the fishy smell of most fish products sold inland) and won't taste good if it is old when it is frozen.

Where to Look for Fruit and Vegetable Bargains

If you are planning to can or freeze only in very small batches, then a bargain is where a sale is, at the local grocery store or supermarket or at a roadside stand.

You can generate bargains by getting together with neighbors to purchase in large quantities. Wholesalers in many cities will sell at wholesale prices to private individuals or groups if they purchase in large quantities. Fruits and vegetables are sold by the bushel, the box, the crate, the peck, the lug box, and the Western box. The legal weight of large bushels of fruits or vegetables varies in different states. How many pounds each of these containers holds depends, of course, on the shape and density of the produce in it. A glance at the tables on pages 19–21 will give you a notion of what to expect.

If you can't find a wholesaler who will sell to you, ask him where he buys his produce and you may be directed to a local suburban or country market gardener who will sell at even better prices than the wholesaler could.

In many suburbs in the Northeast and some areas in the Southwest, big cut-rate food markets operate on the outskirts of urban areas. Here food is sold to the consumer in crates, boxes, bushels, and a quick trip during the picking season of your favorite fruits and vegetables usually yields as much canning and freezing material as you are likely to want.

The other place to look for bargains is in the local newspaper. Today, some local farmers allow the public to pick their own produce— potatoes, apples, and strawberries are a few of the many fruits and vegetables my family has gathered directly from the field. Because you gather the produce yourself, it is the best possible buy for canning or freezing since the produce will be at its freshest as well as low in price.

The best place of all to look for a bargain in fruit and vegetables is in your own or in a neighbor's garden. If you have an urban lot, an apartment, or a condominium (and thus no place for a garden), look for a piece of land in a community garden. All over the country, corporate lands once devoted to other purposes or to ornamental gardening are being offered to employees and local citizens to use to grow food. In cities from New York to California, urban lots slated for future construction are being dug up and used for community gardens. If your community doesn't offer a community garden, scout your neighborhood for a suitable lot, gather bargain-minded gardening friends, and organize to rent the space on a long-term lease.

Where to Find Meat Bargains

The supermarket, the grocery store, and the butcher shop are potential sources of meat bargains, but the best meat bargains generally are found with wholesalers. In large cities, whole districts (see the yellow pages of the telephone book) are devoted to wholesale dispensing of meat and fish, as well as fruit and vegetables. Smaller cities may be without a wholesale meat district, but somewhere within a radius of 50 or 100 miles, there will be a distribution center that dispenses meat to all the cities in the area. Once you've established contact with a wholesaler, you can buy for yourself or for a group of friends to suit your needs and the time available for processing.

Meat wholesalers will give you merchandise at wholesale prices (more or less) if you buy in sufficient quantity. Some wholesalers I have dealt with considered an order for $100 or more as a wholesale order, even though I bought moderate quantities of each of several types of meat and poultry. Other wholesalers (especially when you are new) insist you buy a large amount of a given meat before they will offer you a wholesale price. If you can't make the first type of deal, then organize with neighbors interested in bargain food prices to buy in large lots with you.

How Much Should I Put Up?

This is a hard question to answer, especially for meats, since meat-eating habits are highly individual. As a generalization, 4 to 8 ounces of meat daily per person is considered sufficient nutritionally. But some people like to eat almost a pound of meat at a sitting, and even more are on high-protein diets. Since most of the meat you put up will be frozen, chances are your freezer space will govern how much meat to buy ahead.

Whether to can in pint jars or quart jars is a decision that depends on the amount you are

How Much to Put Up for Each Member of the Family

Food	Number of Times Served	Amount per Person (for 36 weeks)
Citrus fruit and tomatoes (including juices)	seven 1-cup portions per week	63 quarts
Dark green and yellow vegetables (including broccoli, spinach and other greens, carrots, pumpkin, sweet potatoes, and yellow winter squash)	four ½-cup portions per week	18 quarts
Other fruits and vegetables (including apples, apricots, peaches, pears, asparagus, green beans, lima beans, corn, green peas, and summer squash)	seventeen ½-cup portions per week	76 quarts

likely to use at any one meal. Storage in quarts takes less space, and since you're processing twice as much at once in a quart jar, means fewer jars and less time for processing. However, if you have a small family, you may not use a full quart of any given item at one meal, and you'll have to store it in the refrigerator until it can be used.

The table above is based on the U.S. Department of Agriculture's *Daily Food Guide*. It will give you a notion of how much citrus fruit and tomato juice, how many dark green, yel-low, and other vegetables, and how much fruit you might expect to serve in a thirty-six week period for each member of the family.

The two tables on pages 19–21 list the fruits and vegetables that are best for canning and freezing and show how much raw produce is needed to obtain the required number of pints and quarts. Using these three tables, you can work out how much you would like to put up for the eight or so months of the year when fruits and vegetables are most costly, and how much raw produce you will need to buy.

Yield Chart for Canning

Food	If I Buy	I'll Get Pints	Quarts
Applesauce	1 bushel (48 pounds)	30-36	15-18
	2½ to 3½ pounds		1 quart
Apricots	1 box (22 pounds)	14-22	7-11
	2 to 2½ pounds		1 quart
Berries	24 quarts	24-36	12-18
	1½ to 3 pounds		1 quart

Food	If I Buy	Pints	I'll Get Quarts
Cherries	1 box (56 pounds)	44-64	22-32
	2 to 2½ pounds		1 quart
Peaches	1 bushel (48 pounds)	36-48	18-24
	2-3 pounds		1 quart
Pears	1 bushel (50 pounds)	40-50	20-25
	2 to 3 pounds		1 quart
Tomatoes: whole	1 bushel (53 pounds)	30-40	15-20
	2 to 2½ pounds		1 quart
Tomatoes: juiced	1 bushel (53 pounds)	24-32	12-16
	3 to 3½ pounds		1 quart
Beans: lima (in pod)	1 bushel (32 pounds)	12-20	6-10
	2 to 5 pounds		1 quart
Beans: snap	1 bushel (30 pounds)	24-40	12-20
	1½ to 2½ pounds		1 quart
Beets (without tops)	1 bushel (52 pounds)	30-48	15-24
	2 to 3½ pounds		1 quart
Carrots (without tops)	1 bushel (50 pounds)	32-50	16-25
	2 to 3 pounds		1 quart
Corn (in husks)	1 bushel (35 pounds)	12-20	6-10 (whole kernel)
	3 to 6 pounds		1 quart
Okra (baby)	1 bushel (26 pounds)	32-36	16-18
	1 to 1½ pounds		1 quart
Peas (in pods)	1 bushel (30 pounds)	10-20	5-10 (shelled)
	3 to 6 pounds		1 quart
Sweet potatoes	1 bushel (50 pounds)	32-50	16-25
	2 to 3 pounds		1 quart

Yield Chart for Freezing

Food	If I Buy	I'll Get
Apples	1 bushel (48 pounds)	32-40 pints
	1½ pounds	1 pint
Apricots	1 bushel (48 pounds)	60-72 pints
	⅔ pound	1 pint
Asparagus	1 crate (24 pounds)	14-22 pints
	1 to 1½ pounds	1 pint
Beans: lima (in pods)	1 bushel (32 pounds)	12-16 pints
	2 to 2½ pounds	1 pint
Beans: snap	1 bushel (30 pounds)	30-45 pints
	⅔ to 1 pounds	1 pint
Berries	1 crate (24 quarts)	32-36 pints
	1½ pints	1 pint
Broccoli	1 crate (25 pounds)	24 pints
	1 pound	1 pint
Brussels sprouts	4 quart boxes	6 pints
	1 pound	1 pint

Food	If I Buy	I'll Get
Cauliflower	2 medium heads	3 pints
	1½ pounds	1 pint
Chard	1 bushel (12 pounds)	8-12 pints
	1½ pounds	1 pint
Cherries	1 bushel (56 pounds)	36-44 pints
	1½ pounds	1 pint
Collard greens	1 bushel (12 pounds)	8-12 pints
	1½ pounds	1 pint
Corn (in husks)	1 bushel (35 pounds)	14-17 pints
	2 to 2½ pounds	1 pint
Cranberries	1 peck (8 pounds)	16 pints
	½ pound	1 pint
Kale	1 bushel (18 pounds)	12-18 pints
	1 to 1½ pounds	1 pint
Peaches	1 bushel (48 pounds)	32-48 pints
	1½ pounds	1 pint
Peas (in pods)	1 bushel (30 pounds)	12-15 pints
	2 to 2½ pounds	1 pint
Peppers	10 pounds	7 pints
	3 peppers	1 pint
Pineapple	5 pounds	4 pints
Pumpkin	12 pounds	8 pints
	3 pounds	2 pints
Rhubarb	15 pounds	15-22 pints
	1 pound	1 pint
Spinach	1 bushel (18 pounds)	12-18 pints
	1½ pounds	1 pint
Squash: summer	1 bushel (40 pounds)	32-40 pints
	1 to 1½ pounds	1 pint
Squash: winter	12 pounds	8 pints
	3 pounds	2 pints
Strawberries	1 crate (24 quarts)	38 pints
	⅔ quarts	1 pint
Tomatoes: whole	1 bushel (53 pounds)	30-40 pints
	1 to 1½ pounds	1 pint

How Long Will It Take to Put Up?

Preparing enough beans to can for a meal will take about as long as it normally takes to prepare fresh beans for a family meal. Add thirty minutes to an hour for the time it will take to process the jars. Freezing enough beans for a meal will take about as long as it takes you to prepare fresh beans for a family meal, plus ten or twelve minutes for blanching and wrapping. This information doesn't tell you too much, and is offered only to try to give you a ballpark view of the time involved. To answer the question another way, until you get the hang of it, it will probably take you a whole afternoon to put up a bushel of anything. Eventually, once you are sure of each step to take, it will go faster.

Whether you can or freeze the beans, you must wash, sort, snip off ends, and scald or partially cook the beans before you process. In other words, the *preparation* of a bushel of beans for canning or freezing requires only a little more time than if you were preparing to serve them at once. The *processing* doesn't take much effort on your part.

Get the Family Involved

The best way to make canning or freezing in large quantities fun is to avoid trying to put up too much at once.

Make it a neighborhood or a family party. Wives, husbands, and even aunts, uncles, and children are usually fascinated by the "putting up" processes and willing to help—as long as the party is fun. If you decide the whole thing is drudgery and sigh a lot over the time involved, you'll soon find yourself without helpers. Bring in the television set and get everyone to work on the asparagus while watching their favorite show. Serve lemonade, popcorn, and good cheer as a reward for willing work; and you'll find togetherness can be real and the bushel gets done.

One of the happiest ways to can or freeze in small quantities is by planning for leftovers. When peas are in season or you are making your favorite tomato sauce, prepare twice as much as you need for dinner and put it up in cans or in the freezer. It's an easy and practical approach; and if you do it often enough, you'll be amazed at how much you have put up for winter.

Part II
Canning

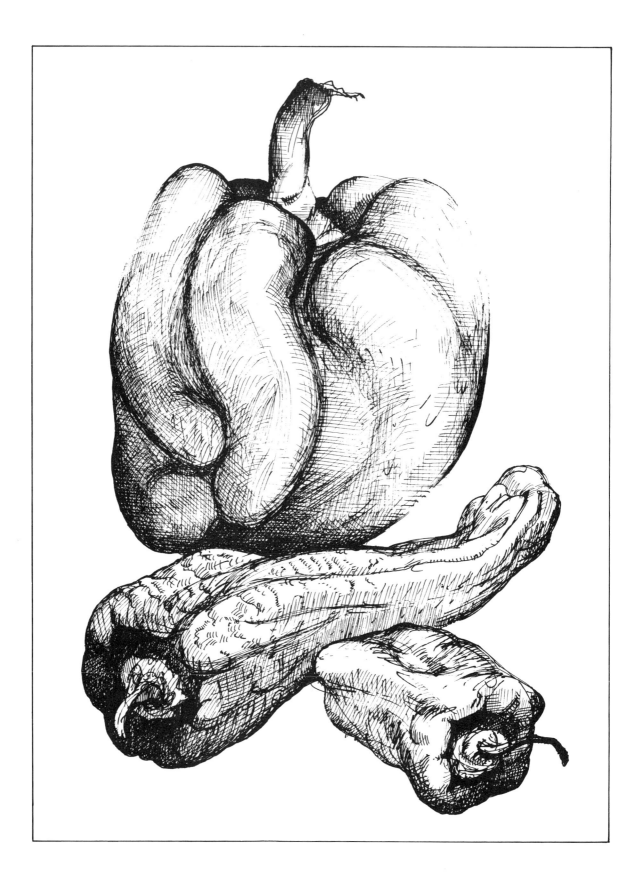

3
What You Have to
Know Before You Can Food

Before you turn your kitchen into a miniature processing plant (a good pastime when inflation has reached you) you should make sure you know about the spoilage of food in jars, and some basic supplies you need.

What Are the Hazards?

There is no danger if you can *properly*, and this means making sure you have processed each food by the method specifically recommended for that food and that you have followed the canning instructions *exactly*. You can be haphazard about the way you slice things to be canned, but you cannot be at all haphazard about the way the food is processed.

Whether in a jar or can, whether in the refrigerator or on a kitchen shelf, foods spoil because they are under constant attack by spoilage organisms—which are always present in the air, water, and soil. Vegetable and fruit enzymes, which help to bring about normal ripening, will continue to ripen the foods until they rot unless they are stopped. When you can vegetables and fruits, you must heat them through at the correct temperature and for the length of time needed to destroy *all* the spoilage organisms to which they are susceptible.

It may be human to want to find shortcuts, but shortcuts in the canning process can be hazardous. Experts on canning—from the U.S.D.A. to the Ball Corporation and the Kerr Glass Manufacturing Corporation, the two biggest suppliers of glass jars for canning—agree that oven canning is not a safe procedure. Not even the new microwave ovens have proved to be safe for oven canning.

Recommendations that you try cold-sealing (which means no processing of the jars after sealing) or cold-sealing after adding aspirin to the jars are considered dangerous nonsense, and only you will be responsible for what may develop in foods handled by such unapproved methods.

Canning powders and chemical preservatives are offered from time to time, but they often are unproven and always are unnecessary if you process foods carefully and correctly.

Foods in jars that have been properly processed, handled, and stored will not spoil. Liquid spurting from containers, gas bubbles, soft, slimy, or moldy food, cloudy liquids, sediment in once-clear liquid, leaking jars, bulging tops, and unnatural colors or odors are signs of imperfectly processed foods. If any of these appear in your canned goods, throw them away. Don't try to salvage the food—it isn't worth the worry!

The most dreaded villain in the roster of hazards of poorly processed canned goods is botulism, a deadly infection caused by *Clostridium botulinum*, a rod-shaped bacterium common to soil all over the world. Plants grown in soil containing this organism could carry the bacterium. In addition, meats from animals that have eaten contaminated plant life could be carriers. This bacterium is harmless in the presence of oxygen, but it multiplies rapidly when oxygen is absent, producing a toxin extremely lethal to man. The toxin has no odor and does not change the appearance of the food. The botulism bacteria do not thrive in high-acid foods, but they do grow and form a toxin in sealed jars of *improperly processed low-acid* foods. The spores are destroyed when the low-acid foods are correctly processed in a steam-pressure canner.

Scary? Sure it is, but no more so than your carving knife. The knife is a lethal weapon, if you make it so. Properly canned, low-acid foods are just fine—grocery store shelves are full of them—it's only if they are improperly canned that you run the risk of botulism.

As you know, especially if you garden, a pH above 7.0 is alkaline; below pH 7.0 is acid. The farther the pH is below 7.0, the higher the acid content. Or to put it in another way, the fruits and vegetables containing the least acid are those with a pH closest to 7.0 and are the ones that have the most sugar or starch content (i.e., are "sweeter"). Spoilage organisms thrive in this low-acid, high-sugar environment unless killed by the canning process.

In canning, foods having a pH between 7.0 and pH 4.6 are considered *low-acid* foods. These foods *must* be pressure processed *at 240°F*. (Chapter 4 describes the pressure canning process and gives recipes for the low-acid foods that must be canned by this

Low-Acid Foods (Above pH 4.4) —Pressure Process at 240°F for time indicated

figs	pH 4.6
pimentos (red peppers)	4.6
pumpkins	5.0
carrots	5.0
cucumbers	5.1
turnips	5.2
cabbage	5.2
squash	5.2
onions	5.2
parsnips	5.3
beets	5.3
snap beans	5.3
sweet potatoes	5.4
spinach	5.5
asparagus	5.6
cauliflower	5.6
mushrooms	5.8
meat	5.8
tuna fish	6.0
potatoes	6.1
peas	6.2
corn	6.3
meat (fresh)	7.0

process.) If you always pressure process foods with a pH above 4.4, botulism is not a problem.

High-acid foods—that is, those with a pH lower than 4.4—need not be processed by pressure canning. These foods can be processed by the boiling water-bath method at 212°F. (Chapter 5 describes the techniques of this method and gives recipes for some of the high-acid foods that are safely canned by this process.) Again let me stress, however, processing at 212°F should only be used for foods with a pH less than 4.4.

The tables below will give you a general idea of the acidity of some of the fruits, vegetables, and meats you are most likely to use for canning. Additional information may be obtained from the Agricultural Extension Service, North Carolina State University, Greensboro, N.C. 27411.

High-Acid Foods (Below pH 4.4) —Process at 212°F

vinegar	pH 2.9 (very acid)
gooseberries	3.0
rhubarb	3.2
dill pickles	3.2
apples	3.2
apricots	3.3
blackberries	3.3
strawberries	3.4
peaches	3.5
plums	3.6
raspberries	3.6
sauerkraut	3.6
blueberries	3.7
sweet cherries	3.8
pears	3.9
tomatoes	4.2

Are There Other Hazards?

Things can go wrong with canning without being health hazards. A look at the list below will suggest some pitfalls and how they can be avoided. In each case, the food in the jar is usable, unless spoilage is indicated. The list was prepared by the Ball Corporation of Muncie, Indiana. Read this list now, and again before you start working with the instructions in Chapters 4 and 5.

Foods Darken in the Top of the Jar: The causes for this could be that (1) the liquid didn't cover the food; (2) the food was not processed long enough to destroy the enzymes; (3) the manner of packing and processing didn't produce a high enough vacuum; (4) air became sealed in the jars either because the head space was too large or the air bubbles weren't removed. You can avoid all these hazards by carefully following the processing instructions in Chapters 4 and 5.

Fruits Darken After They Have Been Taken from the Jar: This can happen if the fruits were not processed long enough to destroy the enzymes. Process each fruit for the recom-

mended length of time. The time is counted from the moment the water reaches a full boil in the boiling-water canner.

Corn Turns Brown: There are several possible causes: (1) the corn was too mature for canning; (2) the liquid didn't cover the corn; (3) the jars were processed at too high a temperature; (4) the variety of the corn was not suitable for canning. To offset these possibilities, be careful to select a variety good for canning. Use freshly picked corn that has plump, shiny kernels. Process it at once. Make sure the corn is covered with liquid before capping the jar, and follow instructions for recommended pressure.

Pink, Blue, Purple Streaks in Apples, Pears, Peaches: These color streaks can be caused by a natural chemical change that occurs in the cooking of the fruit. There's not much that can be done about it.

Green Vegetables Lose Their Bright Color: Heat breaks down the chlorophyl in plants. There's nothing to be done about this, either.

Green Vegetables Turn Brown: This can happen when vegetables are overcooked or when they are too mature for canning. Follow instructions to avoid overcooking and use only very young, fresh vegetables.

Foods Become Black, Brown, or Gray: Tannins, sulphur compounds, and acids in food can react to minerals in the water or with metal utensils used in preparing the foods. If possible, use soft water for canning. Avoid copper, iron, or chipped enamelware and utensils.

Yellow Crystals on Canned Green Vegetables: This is glucoside, a natural and harmless substance found in vegetables. We don't know how to offset it.

White Crystals in Canned Greens: (I prefer not to can greens; however, you may want to.) The white crystals sometimes found on the product are calcium and oxalic acid from the greens, which have combined to form a harmless calcium oxalate. Nothing to be done.

White Sediment in Vegetable Jars: This may denote bacterial spoilage. It also can be caused by starch fallout from the food or by minerals in the water used. If spoilage is there, it will be indicated by liquid that has become murky. *Do not use the food if the liquid is murky.* Bacterial spoilage can be avoided by processing each food by the recommended method and for the recommended length of time. There's nothing you can do about starch fallout, but you can use soft water to avoid mineral fallout.

Fruit Floats in the Jar: This happens when the fruit is lighter than the syrup. It can also happen when the cold-pack method (see page 38) of preparing foods for processing is used. Most of the recipes in this book use the hot-pack method, thus avoiding the problem. To avoid the first problem, use only firm, ripe fruit and use a lighter syrup (see Chapter 5) next time; pack the fruit as closely as possible in the jars.

Cloudy Liquids: This may be a sign of spoiled food—I discard such jars unless I am convinced it has been caused by starch fallout from the food, minerals in the water, or starch fillers in the salt. If the food seems perfectly fine and there are no other signs of spoilage, heat the container for 10 minutes at 212°F. After this, if it looks and smells okay, take a small taste. If it still seems unspoiled, use it. Next time, be sure you use soft water, and try a pure, unrefined salt.

Loss of Liquid During Processing: This can happen. Don't open the jars to replace the liquid and don't be distressed if the food in the jars darkens. You can lose liquid during processing if (1) the food was not heated before packing (one reason I prefer the hot-pack method); (2) the food was not packed tightly enough; (3) air bubbles were not removed before capping the jar; (4) the pressure canner did not operate correctly or the jars were not covered with water in a water-bath canner;

(5) not enough liquid was allowed for absorption by starchy foods. To avoid these hazards, use the hot-pack method and pack the food closely. Remove air bubbles by running a rubber spatula or bottle scraper between the food and the jar. Do not let pressure fluctuate during the processing time. After processing, allow the pressure gauge to drop to zero naturally, and wait an additional 2 minutes before testing the petcock. In water-bath canning, the jars should be covered with 2 inches of water throughout the processing period.

Jar Fails to Seal: This can happen, and you must either correct the cause and reprocess the full time or else use the food inside immediately. Many factors can cause failure of the seal. The most likely are failure to follow the instructions for using jar and cap or that a bit of food has forced its way between the jar and the lid during processing. Which is to say, once again, you must follow instructions in Chapters 4 and 5 exactly.

Jar Seals, Then Comes Open in Storage: Spoilage may be evident, and, if so, don't use the contents. Another possibility is that food particles left on the sealing surface disintegrated. You can avoid this by processing each food by the recommended method and by wiping the sealing surfaces and threads of the jars before capping. Another possibility is a hairfine crack in the jar. Before using, all jars must be thoroughly checked for fine cracks or chips on the rims.

Zinc Caps Bulge: In stored goods, this is usually a sign of spoilage, and the food should be discarded. The cause may be that the cap was screwed on too tightly before processing, a condition which will be evident when the jar is removed from the canner. Another possibility is that the food spoiled from underprocessing. The right way to put on the cap is to screw it tightly, then loosen it about ¼ inch before putting it into the canner (see page 38).

Black Spots on Underside of the Metal Lid: If the jar has been sealed but comes open, this means the food is spoiled, and should be discarded. However, natural compounds in some foods can cause a harmless brown or black deposit on the underside of the lid, and the food is probably safe to eat. To be safe, however, boil at 212°F before using.

How Long Will Canned Goods Last?

Theoretically, canned foods last indefinitely. But in fact they are best used up within a two-year period. Store canned goods in a dry, dark place, at a temperature between 35° and 70°F. Canned goods should not be subjected to freezing, which may soften the texture of the food. However, freezing won't cause spoilage in canned foods unless it breaks the seal or the jar.

If you have any reason to suspect spoilage in canned goods, heat the food at 212°F for 10 minutes before smelling it. If the odor is off, throw the food away. (Spoiled food that is cold may not have an odor.)

Labeling Your Product

Before you begin canning, decide how you want to label your jars. When you've just done a bushel of peaches, you will swear that you'll never have to ask yourself what's in those jars. But six months later you may find it hard to tell them from jars of apricots. Also, it's informative to keep track of which product or method and which syrup or flavoring drew the most applause at the family table.

Name the produce inside the jar and use a label large enough to let you give a few facts: whether these were the apples from your neighbor's tree, from a roadside stand, or those very special apples bought during your Virginia vacation. The date of canning should be on the label too—it will help to remind you to use up the first things first.

Vocabulary of Home Canning

Here's a list of common terms used in canning:

Process, processing: Heating by pressure canner or boiling water bath to kill spoilage organisms.

Cold-pack: Use of uncooked food that is packed into canning jars for processing.

Hot-pack: Use of hot and partially cooked food that is packed into jars for processing.

Pressure canner: A large piece of equipment, a giant pressure cooker, used for processing low-acid foods at 240°F.

Water bath: A method of processing foods in a large kettle of boiling water at 212°F. This method is used for high-acid foods.

Open kettle: The food is fully cooked before processing in a water bath. Jams and jellies are canned by open-kettle method.

Butters: A sweet spread made from pulp of fruit or a combination of fruit and vegetables. The texture is uniform, smooth, and soft. The sugar content may be lower than in jams or jellies.

Chutneys: Condiments made from fruits (or a combination of fruits and vegetables), spices, and acids, such as vinegar or lemon juice. The fruit may be in pieces or puréed.

Conserves: A blend of two or more fruits, also called compotes. Nutmeats and raisins may be added. Fruits may be in shreds, slices, or chunks. Consistency is soft, and any liquid included is a very heavy syrup or a soft jelly.

Jams: A thick, sweet, purée of fruit (or combination of fruit and vegetables) cooked to a soft consistency and containing almost no liquid. The texture varies depending on the fruit and the recipe used.

Jellies: Fruit juice and a sugar syrup cooked together, until sufficiently concentrated to gel when cooled. When turned out of a jar, it should quiver. Jellies contain no pulp or fruit pieces.

Marmalades: Soft fruit jellies containing small pieces of fruit and rind, usually citrus, which are evenly distributed throughout the mixture. Marmalades may be made from a single fruit or from several, and can include vegetables, such as tomatoes and carrots.

Preserves: Whole fruits or large pieces of fruit

preserved in syrup. Fruit should remain plump and tender, and the flavor should not be masked by excessive sugar.

Pickles: Vegetables or fruits conserved in an acid liquid, a saline solution, or alcohol.

Fruit jar: The traditional name for any glass jar made for use in home canning. (See *Mason jar; can or freezer jar.*)

Mason jar: A jar with a screw-thread neck and sloping shoulders. It seals on the top or on a sealing shoulder, depending on the type of cap used.

Can or freezer jar: A tapered, shoulderless jar which is used both for home canning and freezing. It seals on the top with a two-piece metal cap.

Jar cap: Name for any cover used to seal a jar (see pages 38–39).

Dome cap: A two-piece jar cap: a lid and screwband combination. The lid is fitted with a rubber sealing compound, and no other rubber is needed. The lid is used once only. The band may be reused with a new lid.

Zinc cap: One-piece jar cap lined with white porcelain. It is used with Mason jars and rubber rings.

Metal band: A screw-thread band that is used with a metal lid to form a two-piece metal cap.

Jar rubber: A flat rubber ring used as a gasket between a zinc cap and the canning jar.

Low-acid foods: These are foods which contain very little natural acid (see the table, page 26). They must be processed at 240°F for canning for varied lengths of time.

High-acid foods: Foods which contain a percentage of from 0.36 to 2.09, or more, natural acid (see the table, page 27). The term also is applied to foods which are preserved in vinegar; such as tomatoes, sauerkraut, pickles, and relishes.

Venting or exhausting: The action taken when you force air to escape from a jar or when you permit air to escape from a steam-pressure canner.

Vacuum seal: A term applied to airtight jars in which normal atmospheric (air) pressure is absent. When a jar is closed at room temperature, the air pressure is the same inside and outside the jar. When the jar is heated, everything in it expands, forcing out the air, and the air pressure inside the jar becomes less than that outside. When the jar cools, everything in it shrinks, a partial vacuum is formed, and atmospheric pressure of almost 15 pounds per square inch (at sea level) holds the lid down and keeps the jar sealed. The sealing compound on Mason dome lids and the rubber rings used with zinc caps keep the air from going back into the sealed jar.

Supplies You'll Need for Canning

The basic equipment needed for each of the methods of processing canned foods—*pressure canner, water-bath,* and *open kettle*—is described in Chapters 4 and 5. You'll use the same jars for all three methods:

Canning or freezing jars have straight sides, without shoulders, and are sold in ½-pint, 1-pint, and 1½-pint sizes. The ½-pints seal with Mason caps and dome lids and are the sizes to use for jams and relishes you don't expect to use much of at one time. 1-pint and 1½-pint sizes seal with wide-mouth Mason caps with dome lids, and I use these sizes for small batches of fruits and pickles.

Mason jars have sloped shoulders and are sold in pint, quart, and half-gallon sizes. I use the pint sizes for small-sized vegetables, such as young peas, and the quarts for large pickles. The jars seal with either Mason caps with dome lids or with zinc caps and rubber rings.

Wide-mouth Mason jars are sold in quart and half-gallon sizes, and they seal with wide-mouth Mason caps with dome lids.

Small-size quilted crystal jars with decorative caps are usually used for jams and jellies intended for gift giving. These come in small and tall ½-pint sizes and have protective metal coverings. Quilted crystal jars can be used for canning after the original contents are used; seal them with Mason dome caps. They may also be used for freezing and should be handled as described on page 66.

Quilted crystal jelly glasses. These are not meant for processing in a canner. They are sealed with paraffin and the lid serves only as a cover, which does not seal airtight to make a vacuum seal.

Improvised containers are not "illegal" for small, impromptu batches of jellies and marmalades, but should not be used for any serious canning operation. Improvising and using "found materials" is wonderful fun. I use old peanut butter jars as jelly and jam containers. These are sealed with paraffin and don't require vacuum procedures. However, for canning anything else I use regular canning jars, which I know will stand up to the pressure in the pressure canner or won't break in the high temperature of the water bath.

The pressure canner is an essential piece of equipment if you want to can in quart jars. Quart jars, of course, make pressure canning faster because they allow you to process larger batches. Canners (which some manufacturers refer to as cookers) come in sizes ranging from small (called 6-quart) which will hold 7 pint-size standard Mason jars, to very large (called 22-quart) which will hold 20 pints (double-decked) or 7 quart jars.

The main difference between makes of canning equipment lies in the type of gauge used to control pressure. Mirro, one of the biggest manufacturers of home cookers and canners, offers "weight gauge control," while Presto another giant, offers "dial gauge control." Each type offers readings of 5, 10, and 15 pounds. The 15-pound pressure is used primarily for cooking. The 5- and 10-pound pressure readings are intended for canning.

The accuracy of the pressure readings is important in home canning. The U.S. Department of Agriculture recommends that dial pressure gauges be checked annually before any canning gets under way. The County Extension Service Home Economist in your area may be able to refer you to a local source for checking a dial gauge, or give you the address of the manufacturer for checking. The type of gauge called "weight gauge control" does not need annual checking.

CONTAINERS FOR PUTTING FOOD UP: Left: *three straight-sided canning or freezing jars in half-pint, pint, and 1½-pint sizes. Pints and half-pints seal with wide-mouth Mason caps with dome lids.* Right: *first two jars are Mason jars, shown in pint and quart sizes. These Mason jars have sloping shoulders, narrowed mouths, and seal with either Mason caps with dome lids or zinc caps used with rubber rings.* Far right: *a wide-mouth, straight-sided Mason jar. It seals with a wide-mouth Mason cap with a dome lid.*

QUILTED CRYSTAL CANNING CONTAINERS: Left: *a quilted crystal jelly glass, which is sealed with paraffin and is used for jelly only. It is not used with a pressure canner. The lid is only a cover and does not seal airtight, a necessity in a canner.* Right: *a quilted crystal jar for canning. This type may be processed in the pressure canner or boiling water bath. Caps used are Mason dome caps.*

4
The Pressure
Canner Method: Recipes

Most vegetables and meats are low-acid foods and must be canned under steam pressure. If you already have a pressure cooker, you can process some 1-pint jars in it, providing it is the type of pressure cooker that offers a selection of 5, 10, or 15 pounds pressure settings. The 4-quart pressure cooker will accommodate 4 1-pint jars. You might like to work with these smaller batches and sizes for a while before you decide whether you want to invest in the cost of a big pressure canner or cooker.

If you are starting out by canning in a regular pressure cooker instead of a pressure canner, add twenty minutes to the pressure canner time indicated in recipes for pint jars. The reason for this is to compensate for the quick climb the pressure cooker takes at the beginning of the process and for its quick cooling at the end. Do not lower the temperature with cold water, as you generally do when cooking for family meals.

Altitude is an important factor in pressure. Recipes instruct you to process at pressures given for altitudes 2,000 feet or less above sea level. If you live at a higher altitude, use the table below to adjust the pressure and correct the recipe instructions so you'll be sure you never forget. (There's something very exciting about coming home with a glorious buy, and you may be so pleased with yourself you forget the pressure readings in the recipe you are using aren't correct at your altitude—the higher the altitude, the lower the boiling point.) If you are in any question about your altitude, call your local County Extension Service Home Economist.

Altitude Chart

Altitude Above Sea Level	Process at
2,000 to 3,000 feet	12 pounds
3,000 to 4,000 feet	12 pounds
4,000 to 5,000 feet	13 pounds
5,000 to 6,000 feet	13 pounds
6,000 to 7,000 feet	14 pounds
7,000 to 8,000 feet	14 pounds
8,000 to 9,000 feet	15 pounds
9,000 to 10,000 feet	15 pounds

For canners with 5-10-15-lb. weight gauge, use 10 lb. instead of 5 lb. and 15 lb. instead of 10 lb. at altitudes 2,000 feet or higher.

Supplies for Pressure Canning

The only other absolutely essential equipment for pressure canning is the canning jars and lids described in Chapter 3. If you are planning to do sizeable amounts of canning, it is a good idea to buy jars and tops early in the season. It has happened to me more than once that I couldn't find jars after the season began. To know how many jars you are likely to need, look at the tables in Chapter 2 to determine how many pints or quarts you will probably be putting up. Buy whatever number of pint and quart jars you think you will need, plus a few extras to have handy in case you run into something irresistible.

You will also find handy a jar lifter (try the local hardware store for this), a large wide-mouth funnel, and a ladle with a lip. A food mill that will slice or chop is a luxury you'll enjoy, and one that will speed the preparation process greatly—but make sure you really are going to do a lot of canning before you invest in this fairly expensive item. Use only glass, enameled, or heat-resistant plastic equipment since metal in contact with acidity in foods may cause discoloration.

The rest of the equipment used in canning—large measuring cups, large bottles, and trays to hold processed foods while they cool—you probably have on hand or can improvise.

Use pure salt for vegetable canning. It is known as canning or curing salt in some areas, is cheaper than table salt, and it doesn't have either iodine or starch in it. Iodine sometimes causes vegetables to change color, although it doesn't do them any harm. Starch in table salt can cause a white sediment in canned goods that does no harm, but may leave you worried that something is wrong with the food. Besides, the sediment at the bottom of the jar isn't attractive.

Routine Care

Each time before you start pressure canning, clean the petcock and the safety valve on the pressure canner by drawing a string through them, then wash the canner carefully and dry it.

Examine all the jars and lids you are planning to use. Any that are chipped, cracked, or dented should be discarded and replaced. Even the smallest defect can prevent an airtight seal and lead to food spoilage. Nicks on jar tops are easy to overlook, so run your finger around the mouth of each jar to be sure it is whole. Make sure that each jar has a cap with all essential pieces.

EQUIPMENT THAT MAKES HOME CANNING EASY: Pressure canner, at left, is essential for canning low-acid foods. The boiling water-bath canner, at right, is a large kettle used to process foods high in acid content. A 4-cup measuring cup, a wide-mouth funnel, a jar lifter, measuring spoons, a wooden spoon for stirring acid foods, a large stainless spoon for transferring foods, a sharp paring knife, and a timer complete the equipment.

Pressure Canning Step-by-Step

CHECKING JARS BEFORE CANNING: Jar tops with nicks or cracks will prevent airtight sealing of canned foods. Before you start processing, rub your fingertip over the edge of every jar to be used to make sure it is undamaged.

WHAT TO DO WITH THE LIDS: Lids for sealing jars are thoroughly washed in hot soapy water, rinsed, and kept warm in a pan of boiling water.

JARS MUST BE CLEAN: Wash all the jars to be used for each processing before you start preparing foods. Use hot, soapy water. Rinse with boiling hot water.

FILLING THE JARS: Starchy vegetables, such as corn, lima beans, and peas, are packed to 1½ inches from the top of the jar, as shown here at left. Most other foods are packed to within 1 inch of the jar top, as shown at right. Enough boiling liquid to cover the food in the jars is added after packing.

REMOVING AIR BUBBLES FROM THE JARS:
A rubber spatula is used to remove air bubbles that may form on the sides of jars after packing and filling with boiling liquid. The bubbles can cause spoilage of canned goods.

CLOSING THE JARS: *Place the lids on the jars with the sealing composition next to the glass. Screw the screw band on firmly and tighten it before processing foods. These steps are correct for this type of lid; other types of lids are shown on pages 38-39, and instructions are given for closing them.*

WIPING JAR TOPS CLEAN: *Use a damp cloth to remove particles of food remaining on jar threads. These can cause improper sealing of canned goods.*

PROCESSING IN A PRESSURE CANNER: *When the canner is loaded, adjust the lid and fasten it securely. Leave the petcock open for 7 to 10 minutes to exhaust all air from the canner, then close it, watch for the pressure gauge to rise to the desired pressure, and start counting the processing time given in recipes from the moment the pressure reaches the required level.*

TESTING THE SEAL: The easiest way to test the seal of processed jars is to tap the lids with a spoon. A clear, ringing sound means the jar is vacuum sealed. The screw band is then removed. After processing, the seal must be tested and found perfect, or foods will spoil. Other testing methods are described on pages 38-39.

OPTIONAL: Final step in assuring cleanliness of the jars is to wash them after the removal of the screw bands. Wash screw bands carefully so they'll be ready for your next canning venture.

With your equipment ready, and the food to be processed on hand, here are the steps you go through in pressure canning.

Step 1: Estimate how many jars you'll need for one canner load, or all the loads for the day; wash the jars thoroughly in hot, soapy water, or run them through the dishwasher. Keep them hot.

Step 2: Place the lids in a large pan and pour boiling water over them. Don't boil them, but leave them in the water until you are ready to use them.

Step 3: Store vegetables or fruits to be canned in the refrigerator while they are waiting to be prepared for processing. Estimate the amount of food to be processed in one canner load and wash each piece thoroughly in several changes of cold water. (Don't let them soak, unless otherwise instructed, because water dissolves some of the minerals that give them nutritive value.) Lift the vegetables from the washing water, then drain the water, rinsing the bowl to make sure any invisible drifts of sand are gone; repeat this washing step until the fruits or vegetables are absolutely clean.

Step 4: Prepare the vegetables for cooking per the recipe instructions. Sort the vegetables according to size and thickness. For example, big beans and little beans in the same jar don't look good and will cook unevenly. If there is a marked difference in size, divide the sorted vegetables so that each individual batch to be cooked will consist of similarly sized pieces. Measure the quantity that can be fitted into the number of jars the canner will handle at one time.

The right way to work your way through a bushel of vegetables is to prepare only as many vegetables as the pressure canner will process at one time. While the first batch is processing in the canner, prepare the next batch and have it ready for the pressure canner as soon as the first batch is finished.

Step 5: You now have a choice. You can decide to hot-pack the vegetables or cold-pack them. Hot-packing or cold-packing is the step that takes place *before* the cans are sealed and processed. Cold-packed vegetables are placed raw into hot jars; hot-packed vegetables are cooked briefly before packing into hot jars.

There is a tendency for some foods, especially fruits, to float to the top of the jar when the cold-pack method is used. This floating doesn't indicate spoilage, but it looks odd. The hot-pack method ensures a better filling of the jars because air and moisture are released from the food during the heating. Each of the recipes that follows specifies how much time the food should be boiled before processing if the hot-pack method is used.

When you hot-pack, immerse the prepared vegetables or fruit in water that is boiling hard. Do not cover. Let the water return to a boil, and boil for the period of time directed in the recipe. Remove from the water, but do not discard the water.

Step 6: Work fast to keep the food hot. Set the funnel in the mouth of the jar and pour the vegetable pieces into the jar. Bring the cooking water back to a boil, and pour it into the jar, leaving the head space between water top and jar top that is indicated in each recipe. As a generalization, pack starchy vegetables, such as corn and lima beans, to within 1½ inches below the top of the jar, and add boiling water until it reaches 1 inch from the top of the jar. Pack nonstarchy vegetables to within 1 inch from the top of the jar and add enough boiling liquid to leave ½ inch of head space.

Step 7: Run a rubber spatula around the insides of the jars to remove air bubbles. Wipe the jar top and threads clean. Cap the jars as shown in the accompanying sketches and photos. Your pressure canner is fitted with a rack. Just before the food is ready to be packed into the jars, set the pressure canner over medium heat, place the rack in the bottom of the canner, and cover with 1 inch of boiling water in small canners and 2 inches of boiling water in larger canners. As each jar is

When closing this type of canning jar, moisten the rubber ring and place on the shoulder of the jar. Screw the cap down very tightly over the wet ring. Then turn the screw cap back about ¼ inch to loosen it slightly. Process the foods as directed. When you remove the jar from the canner, immediately screw the cap down tightly to complete the seal.

METAL
SCREW BAND
GLASS LID
RUBBER
SEALS HERE

This type of equipment is called "self-sealing." Moisten the rubber ring and place it on the glass lid. Place the lid on the jar with the rubber against the rim of the jar; then put the screw band on and screw it down tightly. Then turn the screw band back ¼ inch to loosen it a little. After processing, and as soon as you remove the jar from the canner, screw the band down tightly to complete the seal.

METAL SCREW BAND

METAL LID

SEALS HERE

When sealing this type of container, put the flat metal lid on the rim of the jar with the sealing side on the glass. Hold the lid down, and screw the band on firmly. Remove the screw band after the seal has been tested, by tapping, as described on page 37.

GLASS LID

WIRE BAIL

RUBBER

SEALS HERE

The lid on this type of canning jar is held down by the wire bail. Moisten the rubber ring and put it on the screw thread at the top of the jar, and press the glass lid on the rubber ring. Then put the lower bail wire over the top of the glass lid so it fits into the groove on the lid. Push the other bail wire down against the side of the jar. The jar is now sealed. Process the jar, and do not disturb the bail wire after processing.

filled and the cap tightened, set it on the rack in the canner to keep hot. Pack only enough jars at one time to fill the canner. Space the jars in the canner so each receives its fair share of steam. Follow the canner instructions carefully to adjust the cover and fasten it securely. Exhaust the canner by leaving the petcock open and letting steam escape freely for seven to ten minutes. Close the petcock. *When the amount of pressure given in the recipe is showing on the pressure gauge, start counting the processing time.* Adjust the heat to keep the pressure steady.

Step 8: Process for the required length of time given in the recipe.

Step 9: When the processing time is up, remove the canner from the heat. Make no effort to lower the pressure. Let the canner stand until the pressure gauge returns to zero. Wait 2 minutes, then open the petcock slowly; if no steam escapes, the pressure is down and the cover can be removed.

Step 10: Remove the jars from the canner (use a jar lifter or a thick oven mitt) and set them upright 2 or 3 inches apart on a rack or on several thicknesses of cloth. Do not set these boiling hot jars on a cold surface or in a cold draft. Do not cover them. Do not tighten the screw bands after processing unless so directed by the manufacturer. Cool about twelve hours.

Step 11: When the jars are cool, test the seal by pressing down on the center of the lid. If the dome is down or stays down when pressed, the jar is sealed. Remove the screw band; wash and save it.

If a jar fails to seal, repack, use a new lid, and reprocess. Or, refrigerate and use as soon as possible.

Step 12: Store in a dry, dark place with temperatures at 70°F or somewhat below.

(Note: Process together in the canner only quarts or only pints. Don't plan to mix the two, as the processing times differ for each. Half-pints and pints require the same processing time and so can be processed together.)

Recipes

Asparagus

Shortly after the season begins, buy tender asparagus with tightly curled tips and fresh-looking cut ends.

Review Steps 1 through 12 on pages 37–39.

1. Wash the asparagus well in two or three changes of water.
2. Use a potato peeler to remove the outer peel up to the tip. Cut away the woody end, at the same time making spears of a size that will allow a 1½-inch head space in the jars you have chosen. Fit the spears into the number of jars you can process at one time in the canner and work only with this amount for each batch.
3. To hot-pack the asparagus, lay them neatly aligned on a rack in the bottom of a large kettle or skillet and cover them with rapidly boiling water. When the water returns to a boil, boil for 3 minutes. Lift the rack from the water and slide the asparagus into the jars which have been laid on their sides. Add ½ teaspoon of salt to each pint jar; 1 teaspoon to each quart jar. Bring the cooking water back to a boil, and fill each jar with boiling water, leaving a 1-inch head space between the water and the top of the jar.
4. Follow Steps 7 through 12 on pages 38–39. Process pints for 25 minutes; process quarts for 30 minutes. Pressure should be at 10 pounds at altitudes up to 2,000 feet above sea level. (If you are at a higher altitude, see the chart on page 34.)

Beans: Lima

Review Steps 1 through 12 on pages 37–39.

1. Wash the beans well and shell them: If the pods are hard to open, plunge them for 1 minute into boiling water, cool, and pull the string tip down hard. Measure out the amount of beans that you will use for each cooking. Prepare only one batch at a time.
2. To hot-pack lima beans, drop them into rapidly boiling water, bring the water back to a boil, and boil rapidly for 3 minutes. Drain, reserve the water, and bring it back to a boil. Pack the beans into hot jars, leaving a 1½-inch head space. Add ½ teaspoon salt to each pint; 1 teaspoon of salt to each quart. Cover with boiling water, leaving a 1-inch head space.
3. Follow Steps 7 through 12 on pages 38–39. Process pints for 40 minutes; process quarts for 50 minutes. If the beans are large, process 10 minutes longer for both pints and quarts. Pressure should be 10 pounds up to altitudes of 2,000 feet. (For higher altitudes, see the Altitude Chart, page 34.)

Beans: Green, Snap, or Wax

Select pencil-slim, crisp beans that snap readily between thumb and forefinger.

Review Steps 1 through 12 on pages 37–39.

1. Wash the beans in several changes of water.
2. Lay beans of similar size and thickness in rows on a cutting board, and cut away each end, making the beans of similar length in the process. Or, cut the beans, after the ends are snipped off, into 2-inch pieces. Fit them into the number of jars your canner can process at one time, and work only with this quantity.
3. To hot-pack beans, drop them into rapidly boiling water, and when the water returns to a boil, boil 3 minutes. Remove the beans from the water. Reserve the water, and bring it back to a boil. Put the beans at once into hot jars, leaving a 1½-inch head space. Add ½ teaspoon salt to each pint jar; 1 teaspoon salt to each quart jar. Cover with boiling water, leaving a 1-inch head space.
4. Follow Steps 7 through 12 on pages 38–39. Process pints for 20 minutes; process quarts for 25 minutes. Pressure must be 10 pounds at altitudes up to 2,000 feet. (For higher altitudes, see Altitude Chart on page 34.)

Beef Stock

Soups, stews, and any gourmet cooking

tastes better when made with homemade beef or chicken stock. This is my favorite recipe for beef stock, but you may add your own flavor touches.

For each 2 quarts of beef stock you will need: 1 pound stewing beef cut into cubes; 2 quarts beef bones with meat on them; 2 teaspoons salt; 8 pepper corns; 2½ quarts water; 2 medium carrots; 2 sprigs parsley; 1 bay leaf; ¼ teaspoon dried thyme.

Review Steps 1 through 12 on pages 37–39.

1. Sprinkle 1 teaspoon of salt in a heavy skillet, and over medium heat brown the beef cubes and the bones on all sides. Pour a little water into the skillet, scrape up the pan juices, and turn the skillet contents into a large, heavy kettle. Place all remaining ingredients in the kettle, adding enough cold water to cover—about 2½ quarts; bring the water to a boil over high heat, then lower the heat, cover and simmer for 6 hours. Taste the broth; if it seems weak, add more salt; if it still seems insipid, remove the lid of the kettle and boil rapidly until water is reduced and flavor stronger.
2. Drain the boiling stock into hot canning jars, filling to within 1 inch of the top of the jar. (Serve the boiled beef and carrots with horseradish for dinner. It's a French peasant delicacy.)
3. Follow Steps 7 through 12 on pages 38–39. Process both pint and quart jars for 45 minutes, at a pressure of 10 pounds for altitudes up to 2,000 feet. (See Altitude Chart on page 34 for higher altitudes.)

Beets

Select beets no more than 2 or 3 inches in diameter. Freshness of beet tops will tell you how old the beets are.

Review Steps 1 through 12 on pages 37–39.

1. Trim away leaves, leaving 2 inches of stem and the tap root at the other end. Separate the beets according to size, and prepare only the amount that can be processed in your canner at one time. Wash the beets in several changes of water.
2. In a big kettle full of rapidly boiling water, boil each size of beet as a separate group until the outer skin slips off easily, 20 minutes or more, depending on the size and freshness of the vegetables.
3. Remove the skins, cut the tops down to the beet globes, and remove the tap roots. Slice, dice, or pack whole into hot jars, leaving a 1½-inch head space. Fill the jars with boiling beet water, leaving a 1-inch head space. Add ½ teaspoon salt to each pint jar; 1 teaspoon to each quart jar.
4. Follow Steps 7 through 12 on pages 38–39. Process pints for 30 minutes; process quarts for 35 minutes. Add 10 minutes more if beets have been packed whole. Pressure should be at 10 pounds for altitudes up to 2,000 feet. (See Altitude Chart on page 34 for higher regions.)

Carrots

Select baby carrots 4 to 6 inches in length, with fresh tops.

Review Steps 1 through 12 on pages 37–39.

1. Remove the carrot tops, and wash the carrots thoroughly. Scrape with a knife or a potato peeler. Rinse.
2. Grade the carrots according to size and thickness, and plan to process in separate batches all those of similar size. Fit the carrots into the number of jars the canner will process, and work with these.
3. To hot-pack, drop the carrots into a large kettle full of boiling water, bring the water back to a boil, and boil 3 minutes. Remove the carrots from the water. Reserve the water and bring it back to a boil. Pack the carrots neatly into the jars, leaving a 1-inch head space. Add ½ teaspoon of salt to each quart jar. Cover with boiling water, leaving a ½-inch head space.
4. Follow Steps 7 through 12 on pages 38–39. Process pints 25 minutes; quarts 30 minutes. Pressure must be 10 pounds up to 2,000 feet altitude. (See the Altitude Chart on page 34 for higher altitudes.)

Cauliflower

Review Steps 1 through 12 on pages 37–39.

1. Cut the florets from the main stalks and into pieces about 2 inches long, and soak them in a light brine (1 teaspoon of salt to each quart of water) for 30 minutes.
2. Measure how much you'll be able to pack into the number of jars your canner can hold at one time.
3. To hot-pack, drop the florets into a kettle full of rapidly boiling water, and when the water returns to a boil, boil for 3 minutes. Remove the cauliflower from the water; reserve the water and bring it back to a boil. Pack the florets into hot jars, heads up, leaving a 1-inch head space. Cover with boiling water, leaving a ½-inch head space.
4. Follow Steps 7 through 12 on pages 38–39. Process pints for 30 minutes; quarts for 35 minutes. Pressure must be at 10 pounds for altitudes up to 2,000 feet. (See the Altitude Chart for regions higher than 2,000 feet above sea level on page 34.)

Celery and Tomatoes

Celery by itself is hardly worth canning because it is available at reasonable prices throughout the year. Canned with tomatoes, however, it makes a good table vegetable when drained and cooked in butter, as well as a good base for soups and stews. To fill 8 quart jars, you'll need 32 cups of vegetables: 12 cups celery in 1-inch pieces; 12 cups chopped tomato; 4 cups peeled and coarsely chopped onions; and 4 cups peeled, seeded, and coarsely chopped green peppers.

1. Wash, cut away bruises, peel, core, and prepare the vegetables listed above.
2. Put all the vegetables into a large, heavy kettle, turn the heat to medium, add 8 teaspoons of salt, 4 minced cloves of garlic, and cover. When the liquid in the kettle begins to boil, stir gently, and keep at simmer for 5 minutes.
3. Pack into hot jars, leaving 1 inch of head space; if the jars aren't quite filled, add enough boiling water to each to bring the level to within ½ inch of the top of the jar.
4. Follow Steps 7 through 12 described on pages 38–39. Process quarts for 35 minutes.

If you can in pints, process also for 35 minutes. Pressure should be at 10 pounds up to 2,000 feet altitudes. (For higher altitudes, see the chart on page 34.)

Chicken Stock

As with homemade beef stock, all recipes taste better with your own homemade broth. To make chicken stock you will need *for each 2 quarts:* 2½ pounds of chicken or chicken parts; 2 quarts cold water; 1 small onion, peeled; 1 medium carrot, scraped; 1 parsnip, peeled; 2 cloves garlic, peeled; 6 black peppercorns; 2 sprigs parsley; 1 bay leaf; ¼ teaspoon dried thyme; salt. (Note: for a more Italian flavor, 1 teaspoon rosemary may be substituted for the parsley, bay leaf, and thyme.)

Review Steps 1 through 12 on pages 37–39.

1. Place all the ingredients in a large kettle over high heat. When the water boils, lower the heat and simmer, covered, for 4 hours. After 4 hours if the flavor is insipid, boil down until it suits you but add a little salt first to make sure lack of salt isn't the problem. Remove the chicken meat from the bones, and distribute among the canning jars. Strain the stock, and fill the jars to within 1 inch of the top.
2. Follow Steps 7 through 12 on pages 38–39. Process both quart and pint jars for 45 minutes at 10 pounds pressure at altitudes up to 2,000 feet. (For higher altitudes, see the Altitude Chart, page 34.)

Corn: Whole Kernel

Use only freshly picked, young, sweet corn of a variety good for canning.

Review Steps 1 through 12 on pages 37–39.

1. Husk the corn, wash the ears, and remove all the silk. Dry the ears. Hold the ears end up on a cutting board, and with a very sharp knife cut the kernels from the cob, close to the cob. Don't scrape the cob. Prepare only enough kernels to fill the number of jars your canner will process at one time.
2. Place the kernels in a large kettle and cover

with boiling water. As soon as the water returns to a boil, drain the kernels; reserve the water and bring it to a boil. Fill the canning jars with the drained corn to within 1½ inches of the top. Add ½ teaspoon of salt to each pint; 1 teaspoon to each quart. Fill to within 1 inch of the top with the boiling corn-cooking water or additional boiling water.

3. Follow Steps 7 through 12 on pages 38–39. Process pints 55 minutes; process quarts 1 hour and 25 minutes. Pressure should be 10 pounds at altitudes up to 2,000 feet. (See the Altitude Chart, page 34, for regions above 2,000 feet.)

Corn: Cream-Style

Less perfect ears of corn can be used to make cream-style corn. Can only in pint jars.

Follow the instructions for making Whole Kernel Corn (page 42), but instead of cutting kernels close to the cob cut the kernels about halfway to the cob. With a knife, press the meat from the kernels remaining on the cob. Boil the corn with just enough water to cover for 3 minutes, then pack into pint jars, leaving 1½-inches head space. Add ½ teaspoon of salt per jar. Fill the jars to within 1 inch of the top with cooking liquid or additional boiling water. Process the jars 85 minutes at 10 pounds pressure in atlitudes up to 2,000 feet. (See the Altitude Chart on page 34 for higher altitudes.)

Mixed Vegetables

Diced carrots and cut green beans, or peas and diced carrots, and other vegetables mixes can be canned together, though I prefer these mixes frozen. To make vegetable mixes, prepare each vegetable as described for hot-packing, then combine them.

1. Pack the vegetables into hot jars, leaving a 1-inch head space, cover with cooking water, leaving ½-inch head space.
2. Follow Steps 7 through 12 on pages 38–39. Process quarts and pints for that period of

time required by the vegetable of the pair that requires the *longest* processing. Process at the pressure called for by the vegetable requiring processing at the *highest* pressure.

Okra and Tomatoes

A good vegetable mix is half tomato and half okra, especially if you can find fresh, young okra.

Review Steps 1 through 12 on pages 37–39.

1. Wash and stem the tomatoes. Wash the okra, break off the stems, cover with boiling water for 1 minute, then drain and dry. Then cut the okra and tomatoes into pieces of similar size. Prepare a large enough quantity to fill the number of jars your canner can hold at one time.
2. Place tomato and okra pieces in a large, heavy kettle over low heat, and heat until the juices are rendered and begin to boil. Lower the heat and simmer a full 3 minutes.
3. Pack into hot jars to within 1 inch of the top. If you don't have quite enough to fill the jars, add enough boiling water to bring the contents to within ½ inch of the top.
4. Follow Steps 7 through 12 on pages 38–39. Process pint jars for 25 minutes, quart jars for 40 minutes, at 10 pounds pressure at altitudes up to 2,000 feet. (For higher altitudes, see the Altitude Chart on page 34.)

Onions

Canned onions are excellent, though perhaps not quite as good as frozen onions. However, it's so convenient to have them handy to cream or add to a stew without going to all the trouble of peeling them that, whether canned or frozen, they are well worth putting up. And your own will taste better than the commercially processed product. Use small white onions.

Review Steps 1 through 12 on pages 37–39.

1. Peel the onions under running water, and measure the quantity that your canner can process in one batch.

2. Place the onions in a large kettle full of boiling water, bring the water back to a boil, and boil 5 minutes. Remove the onions from the water. Reserve the water and keep it at a boil. Pack the onions into hot jars leaving 1 inch of head space. Fill the jars with the boiling onion water to within ½ inch of the top.
3. Follow Steps 7 through 12 on pages 38–39. Process both quart and pint jars for 40 minutes at 10 pounds pressure in altitudes up to 2,000 feet. (If at higher altitudes, see the Altitude Chart, page 34.)

Peas: Green

Canned green peas don't taste as much like fresh peas as do frozen green peas, but they have a very special flavor of their own, and they are excellent with fish and seafood. You can can them alone or combine them with tiny white onions or with thin slices of larger onions.

Review Steps 1 through 12 on pages 37–39.

1. Shell the peas, and divide them into two groups, large and small. Measure out as many as your canner can process at one time. Peel one onion, about 1½ inches in diameter, for each quart jar to be packed. Or, cut a large peeled onion into thick slices, one slice for each jar. Use proportions equivalent to one onion 1½ inches diameter for each 4 cups of peas.)
2. Place the smaller peas and the onions or onion slices in a large kettle, and cover with boiling water. Bring the water back to a boil, and boil 3 minutes. At the same time, place the larger peas in a large kettle, along with their proportion of onions, cover with boiling water, bring the water back to a boil, and boil for 5 minutes. When the small peas are ready, remove them from the water, along with the onions, and pack them into hot jars. Repeat the process with the large peas as soon as they are done. Leave 1-inch head space in the jars, and cover with the cooking water, which should still be boiling,

filling the jars to within ½ inch of their tops.
3. Follow Steps 7 through 12 on pages 38–39. Process pints 40 minutes and quarts 40 minutes, each at 10 pounds pressure for altitudes up to 2,000 feet. (For higher altitudes, see the Altitude Chart, page 34.)

Pimento

Pimento peppers put up in pint jars make a wonderful addition to Italian dishes and to summer salads. Select ripe, red, sound peppers.

Review Steps 1 through 12 on pages 37–39.

1. Wash the peppers and place them in boiling water for 12 to 15 minutes, then remove the peppers, dip them briefly in cold water, skin them, remove the stems and the seeds.
2. Place the pimentos, flattened, in layers in pint jars, and pack to within ½ inch of the top. These are dry-packed, so don't add water or oil.
3. Follow Steps 7 through 12 on pages 38–39. Process the jars for 10 minutes at 10 pounds pressure at altitudes up to 2,000 feet. (See the Altitude Chart, page 34, if you are in a higher region.)

Succotash

Succotash is a mixture of corn and lima or shell beans that almost everyone loves. It is delicious both canned and frozen.

Review Steps 1 through 12 on pages 37–39.

1. Shell 10 or 12 cups of lima or shell beans for each 20 ears of corn. Husk, remove the silk, and wash the corn. Cover it with boiling water, and boil 5 minutes. Remove the corn, reserving the water. Holding the cobs upright, cut the kernels cleanly from the cob with a sharp knife. Do not scrape the cobs. Measure the corn in cups. Measure two-thirds the amount of lima beans or fresh shell beans. Place the beans in the water the corn boiled in, adding more if necessary to bring the water to a level that covers the beans. Boil the beans 3 minutes.
2. Mix the corn and the beans, and pack into hot jars; leave 1½-inches head room. Bring

the cooking water back to a boil, and fill the jars, leaving 1-inch head space. (Add more boiling water if needed.) Add ½ teaspoon of salt to each pint jar; 1 teaspoon to each quart jar.

3. Follow Steps 7 through 12 on pages 38–39. Process pint jars for 1 hour; process quarts for 1 hour and 25 minutes. Pressure should be 10 pounds at altitudes up to 2,000 feet. (See the Altitude Chart, page 34, for higher regions.)

Sweet Potatoes

Although some canners process sweet potatoes in what is called "dry-pack" without any liquid at all, others like me prefer them canned in a medium syrup.

Review Steps 1 through 12 on pages 37–39.

1. Select sweet potatoes of similar size and thickness, and gauge how many can be processed at one time. Wash thoroughly. Boil for 20 minutes, and remove the skins (they should slip off easily). Cut the potatoes into medium pieces, or, if they are small, leave them whole.
2. While the potatoes are cooking, prepare the syrup on pages 49–50.
3. Drain and pack the potatoes hot into hot jars, leaving 1-inch head room. Fill the jars to within ½ inch of the top with the syrup, which should be boiling hot.
4. Follow Steps 7 through 12 on pages 38–39. Process pint jars 55 minutes, and quarts 90 minutes, at 10 pounds pressure at altitudes up to 2,000 feet. (For higher altitudes, see the chart, page 34.)

5
Canning with Boiling Water Bath: Recipes

Fruits, tomatoes, and other foods that are high in acid content (that is, those with a pH lower than 4.4) are prepared in much the same manner as foods low in acid content, but they can be processed at lower temperatures and do not require a pressure canner. If you are just beginning your career as a canner, you might like to investigate canning this way for your first efforts. It's called a *boiling water bath*, or *water-bath canning*.

On pages 10–13 you will find a list of the fruits and vegetables that can be canned by the boiling water-bath method. At the end of this chapter are recipes for these foods.

The equipment you need, aside from the usual jars, covers, and utensils described on pages 30–31, is a large, very deep kettle with a lid. Water-bath canners are available on the market, but any large container can be used as a boiling water-bath canner if it is deep enough so that the water comes at least 2 to 4 inches *over* the tops of the jars being processed and has enough space to boil freely. The canner must have a tight-fitting cover and a wire or wooden rack on the bottom on which the jars will rest. (The jars must not rest on the bottom of the kettle.)

If you already have a steam pressure canner, you can use that as a boiling water-bath canner provided it is deep enough. Leave the petcock open so that steam escapes and pressure doesn't build up inside during the boiling water bath.

The water-bath canner sold commercially is a large kettle with a cover and rack or metal basket which may or may not have divisions that keep the jars well separated.

Altitudes Affect Processing Time in the Water-Bath Canner

Altitude is an extremely important consideration in water-bath canning because it governs the temperature at which water will boil. Since a water-bath canner doesn't have a pressure gauge, timing must be adjusted. The chart below shows how to increase processing time given in the recipes to suit the altitude where you live.

Water-Bath Canner Altitude Chart
Increase Processing Time above Sea Level

Altitude	For recipe of 20 minutes or less at sea level, add:	More than 20 minutes, add:
1,000 feet	1 minute	2 minutes
2,000 feet	2 minutes	4 minutes
3,000 feet	3 minutes	6 minutes
4,000 feet	4 minutes	8 minutes
5,000 feet	5 minutes	10 minutes
6,000 feet	6 minutes	12 minutes
7,000 feet	7 minutes	14 minutes
8,000 feet	8 minutes	16 minutes
9,000 feet	9 minutes	18 minutes
10,000 feet	10 minutes	20 minutes

Steps in Boiling Water-Bath Canning

With your equipment ready, as described in Chapter 3, and the food to be processed on hand, here are the steps you must follow in water-bath canning. They are similar to those for pressure canning, pages 37–39.

Step 1: Estimate how many jars you will need for each canning load. Wash the jars thoroughly, and keep them hot.

Step 2: Place the lids in a pan, cover them with boiling water, and leave them there.

Step 3: Wash the fruits or vegetables well.

Step 4: Prepare them for canning, as described in the recipes.

Step 5: Grade them according to size, and measure the quantities that will fit into the jars the water-bath canner will hold in a single batch. Work only on one batch at a time. (While the first batch is cooking, prepare the fruits and vegetables for the second batch; and so on.)

Step 6: If the food is to be packed in syrup, prepare the syrup. (See recipes below.)

Step 7: Boil the fruits or vegetables as described in the recipes. This is the hot-pack method, and the one I recommend for most canning processes.

Step 8: Pack the jars, and fill with the syrup or boiling water, as specified in the recipes.

Step 9: Run a rubber spatula around the insides of the jars to remove air bubbles. Wipe the threads and the jar tops clean. Cap as shown in the sketches on pages 38–39.

Step 10: Set the rack in the water-bath canner, and half-fill the canner with boiling water. As each jar is packed and sealed, place it on the rack in the canner. When all the jars are in, pour very hot water down the *sides* of the canner (not over the tops of the jars) to cover the tops of the jars 2 to 4 inches. Put the cover on the canner.

Step 11: Bring the water to a boil. At altitudes of up to 1,000 feet above sea level, process pints for about twenty-five minutes, quarts thirty minutes. (See individual recipes for instructions.) The water should be maintained at a steady, gentle boil.

Step 12: Remove the jars from the canner, and set on racks or towels, away from cold drafts, for twelve hours to cool. Test for seal, as shown on page 37, and then remove the screw bands and store without bands.

Preparing Fruits for Water-Bath Canning

Apples, apricots, peaches, and pears may change color after they are peeled. To avoid this, drop them as they are peeled and cored into a solution of 2 tablespoons each of salt and vinegar to 1 gallon of water. Do not leave them there for longer than twenty minutes, or they will absorb the flavor of the solution. Or you can use a mixture of ascorbic acid (vitamin C) and citric acid combined with water. These acids are sold at drugstores and hardware stores. Follow the manufacturer's instructions.

Fruits sometimes change color in the jars, and many canners use a solution of ascorbic and citric acid to prevent this possibility. If you are using pure ascorbic acid, sprinkle ¼ teaspoon to each quart over the fruit in the jar just before capping. If you are using a mixture of ascorbic and citric acid, follow the manufacturer's instructions.

Syrups for Canned Fruits

Syrups used for canning are rated as light, medium, or heavy. Depending on your taste preferences and nutritional beliefs, these syrups can be made with sugar and water; sugar, honey, and water; or sugar, corn syrup, and water. A honey syrup of *medium* consistency is made using 1 cup of sugar and 1 cup of honey to 4 cups of water. *Medium* syrup using corn syrup calls for 1½ cups of sugar and 1 cup of corn syrup to 3 cups of water.

To make any of these syrups, measure the sugar (or the sugar combined with honey or corn syrup) into a saucepan, add the water, and simmer until the sugar dissolves. Keep the syrup hot until it is needed, but don't let it boil down.

BOILING WATER-BATH CANNER: The water-bath canner is a very large, very deep kettle used to process foods high in acid content. The sketch shows its essential features: a rack is necessary to keep glass jars from resting on bottom of canner; the canner must be deep enough to allow at least 2 inches of space above jar tops for boiling water; canner must have close-fitting lid to keep water boiling evenly.

REMOVING PROCESSED JARS FROM A WATER-BATH CANNER: After processing in boiling water-bath canner, jars are removed with the help of a jar lifter, and set to cool on a rack or on towels, away from cold drafts. Cool for about 12 hours. When cool, remove screw bands, test for seal, clean jars, and store.

Sugar and Water Syrups for Canning

	Sugar	Yield of Syrup
Light	2 cups per 1 quart water	5 cups
Medium	3 cups per 1 quart water	5½ cups
Heavy	4¾ cups per 1 quart water	6½ cups

How Much Syrup Will You Need?

Usually, 1 to 1½ cups of syrup is required for each quart of fruit. If you want to know exactly how much syrup you will need for a given batch of fruit, pack the prepared fruit into the canning jars, fill each jar with water, pour out the water and measure how much it totals. Then make that much syrup.

Recipes

Apple Rings: Spiced

Review Steps 1 through 12 on pages 48–49.

1. Wash the apples, core and peel them, and· slice into rings ¼ to ½ inch thick. Drop into ascorbic acid mixture as they are peeled (see page 49). Measure enough rings to fill the number of jars you will process at one time, and enough syrup to fill the jars, about 1 to 1½ cups for each quart jar. Add to the syrup 5 or 6 drops of red food coloring, enough to make the syrup a dark, rich red. Add ½ teaspoon of cinnamon powder for each cup of syrup. Put the rings into the hot syrup, bring the syrup back to a boil, and simmer 3 to 5 minutes.
2. Remove the rings, pack into hot jars to within 1 inch of tops. Fill jars to within ½ inch of the tops with boiling cooking syrup.

3. Follow Steps 9 through 12 (pages 48–49). Process pints for 20 minutes, quarts 25 minutes at altitudes of up to 1,000 feet. (See the Altitude Chart on page 48 for higher regions.)

Applesauce

To make about 4 pints of applesauce, you will need 20 large, firm apples, preferably very tart.

Review Steps 1 through 12 on pages 48–49.

1. Wash and core the apples, and remove any bruised spots. Drop the peeled apples into ascorbic acid solution (see page 49) as they are cored.
2. When all the apples are ready, remove them from the solution and rinse well. Quarter them, and simmer over medium heat in 4 cups of water until soft. Mash them in the water with a potato masher. Add 2½ cups sugar and 2 teaspoons of cinnamon (if desired). Return to a boil.
3. Pack the sauce into hot jars to within ½ inch of the tops.
4. Follow Steps 9 through 12 on pages 48–49, making very sure the jar threads and tops are thoroughly clean. Process pints 25 minutes, quart jars 25 minutes, at altitudes up to 1,000 feet. (See the Altitude Chart on page 48 for higher regions.)

Apricots: Whole

Review Steps 1 through 12, pages 48–49.

1. Measure the number of fresh apricots needed to fill the jars you can process in the canner at one time. Wash and scald the apricots to facilitate removal of skins. Remove the pits, and place the fruit in ascorbic acid solution (page 49) while pitting remaining fruits.
2. Make enough syrup to fill the jars, plus 2 cups more. A medium or light syrup is suitable for apricots. (I prefer medium.)
3. Remove the apricots from the ascorbic solution, rinse well, and place several at a time

in the syrup, which should be boiling lightly. Boil each batch 3 to 5 minutes and pack into hot jars, leaving 1-inch head space. Cover the apricots in the jars with the boiling syrup to within ½ inch of the jar tops.

4. Follow Steps 9 through 12, pages 48–49. Process pints for 25 minutes, quarts for 30 minutes, at altitudes up to 1,000 feet. (For higher regions, see the Altitude Chart on page 48.)

Berries

Cold-pack berries like raspberries that do not hold their shape well.

Review Steps 1 through 12, pages 48–49.

Cold-Pack Method for Raspberries and Soft Berries

1. Stem or hull the berries, picking out any that are mashed or mildewed, and wash them quickly in ice cold water. Drain well.
2. Measure the amount of berries needed to fill the jars to be processed, and make enough light or medium syrup (depending on whether you like things sweet) to fill the jars, about 1 to 1½ cups per jar.
3. Pour ½ cup of boiling hot syrup into each jar, and fill jar with berries. Shake the jars as you add the berries to pack them well without crushing them. Leave ½-inch head space. Add enough more boiling syrup to fill the jars to within ½ inch of rim.
4. Follow Steps 9 through 12, pages 48–49. Process pints for 15 minutes, quarts for 20 minutes.

Hot-Pack Method for Firm Berries:

1. Wash, drain, and measure the berries. Place berries in a large kettle with ¼ to ½ cup of sugar for each quart of berries. Let stand for 2 hours, then cook, stirring constantly, over slow heat until the sugar dissolves and the berries are boiling hot, about 2 minutes. Do not overcook.
2. Pour the hot berries immediately into hot jars, leaving a ½-inch head space. Cover with syrup, or add a little extra boiling water to within ½ inch of the jar tops.
3. Follow Steps 9 through 12, pages 48–49.

Process pints for 10 minutes, quarts for 15 minutes, at altitudes up to 1,000 feet. (See Altitude Chart, page 48, for timing in higher regions.)

Cherries

Both sweet and sour cherries are processed this way. If the cherries are sweet, make a light or medium syrup. If they are sour, make a medium or heavy syrup. Sour cherries for pies may be canned in water, but lose their color.

Review Steps 1 through 12, pages 48–49.

1. Wash, drain, and stem the cherries; pit them, if desired. (If the pits are left in, prick each cherry with a sterilized needle to prevent bursting.)
2. Measure the cherries you will need to fill the jars to be processed for one cooking, and prepare enough syrup to fill the jars plus 1 cup.
3. Boil the cherries in the syrup 1 to 2 minutes, or just enough to thoroughly scald them. Remove the cherries and pack into hot jars, leaving ½-inch head space.
4. Fill the jars with the hot cooking syrup, leaving ½-inch head space. Add boiling water if you run out of syrup.
5. Follow Steps 9 through 12, pages 48–49. Process pints for 10 minutes, quarts for 15 minutes, at altitudes up to 1,000 feet. (See Altitude Chart, page 48, for higher regions.)

Cranberry Sauce

Instructions for freezing whole cranberries are given in the freezing section, but it's fun to make cranberry sauce to give away at Christmas. To make 2 pints of cranberry sauce, you will need 1 quart of fresh cranberries, 1 cup of water, and 2 cups of sugar.

Review Steps 1 through 12, pages 48–49.

1. Wash and pick over the cranberries. Place them in a kettle, and add 1 cup of water. Cook over low to medium heat, stirring until the berries are soft, about 5 minutes, or until berries begin to pop. Press through a sieve. Return the sieved mixture to the

kettle, add 2 cups of sugar, and simmer until the sugar dissolves, about 3 minutes. Pack into hot jars, leaving ½-inch head space.

2. Follow Steps 9 through 12, pages 48–49. Process both quarts and pints for 10 minutes at altitudes up to 1,000 feet. (Consult the Altitude Chart, page 48, for processing time in higher regions.)

Peach Halves

Review Steps 1 through 12, pages 48–49.

1. To estimate how many peaches you can process in one load, place whole peaches in your canning jars. Then add a few more. You are going to halve them, and the jars will hold more halved peaches than whole ones.
2. Wash the peaches, and dip them briefly in boiling water to facilitate skinning. If you have trouble skinning them, peel them with a potato peeler. As they are peeled, drop them into an ascorbic acid mixture, (page 49) while you finish the batch. When finished, rinse the peaches well in cold water and cut them into halves and pit them.
3. Prepare enough medium syrup for the number of jars you will be using—1 to 1½ cups syrup per quart—and simmer the peach halves, several at a time, in the syrup for about 3 minutes. Pack into hot jars, leaving 1-inch head space.
4. Fill the jars with boiling syrup, leaving ½-inch head space.
5. Follow Steps 9 through 12, pages 48–49. Process pints for 20 minutes, quarts for 25 minutes, at altitudes up to 1,000 feet. (See Altitude Chart, page 48, for higher regions.)

Pears

Bartlett pears are considered best for canning. If those you buy aren't fully ripe, store them at 60° to 65°F until ripe, but not soft.
Review Steps 1 through 12, pages 48–49.

1. Halve the pears and core them, then peel them and drop them into an ascorbic acid mixture (page 49) to keep them from discoloring while you finish the batch. Prepare only as many as your canner can process in one batch.
2. Prepare a light syrup: 1½ cups for each quart jar to be filled, plus 2 cups.
3. Drain the pears, rinse them well in cold water, and drop them into the boiling syrup. Cook 5 minutes, then remove to hot jars. Pack the jars to within 1 inch of the tops. Fill with boiling syrup to within ½ inch of the tops.
4. Follow Steps 9 through 12, pages 48–49. Process pints for 20 minutes, and quarts for 25 minutes, at altitudes of up to 1,000 feet. (For higher regions, consult the Altitude Chart, page 48.)

Cinnamon Pears

Follow the procedures in the preceding recipe, but add 2 sticks of cinnamon and 6 to 8 drops of red food coloring to each quart of syrup. Remove the cinnamon before packing the pears.

Mint Pears

Follow the procedures for canning Pears, but add 6 drops of oil of peppermint (or more, if desired) to each quart of syrup, plus enough green food coloring to turn the syrup a dark, rich green. Cook the pears in the syrup 10 minutes before packing.

Plums

Select small, firm plums.
Review Steps 1 through 12, pages 48–49.

1. Wash the plums, measure how many you'll need to fill the number of jars to be processed at one time, then prick the plums with a sterilized needle to prevent bursting.
2. Prepare amount of medium syrup needed to fill the number of jars to be processed: 1 to 1½ cups of syrup per quart, plus 2 cups.
3. Dry the plums and simmer them in the syrup for 2 minutes. Pack them into hot

jars to within 1 inch of the tops.

4. Fill the jars with boiling syrup, leaving ½-inch head room.

5. Follow Steps 9 through 12, pages 48–49. Process pints for 20 minutes, quarts for 25 minutes, at altitudes up to 1,000 feet. (See the Altitude Chart on page 48 for higher regions.)

Rhubarb

Select slender, crisp, red rhubarb stalks with fresh foliage.

Review Steps 1 through 12, pages 48–49.

1. Remove the foliage, and wash the stalks. Cut the stalks into 1½-inch pieces, and add ½ cup of sugar (or 1 whole cup if you have a sweet tooth) for each quart of rhubarb pieces. Mix and let stand 3 or 4 hours at room temperature.

2. Place the rhubarb in a large kettle over low heat, and heat until the juices are rendered and the liquid is simmering. Boil ½ minute.

3. Pack at once into hot jars, leaving ½-inch head room.

4. Follow Steps 9 through 12, on pages 48–49. Process both pints and quarts for 10 minutes at altitudes up to 1,000 feet. (In higher regions, see Altitude Chart, page 48.)

Tomatoes: Whole

You will need about 1½ cups of extra tomato juice per quart jar for this recipe. The type of tomato you use governs the amount of time required for processing. Red tomatoes require 35 minutes to process per pint, and 45 minutes to process per quart. The pink, orange, and yellow tomatoes (called "low-acid") must be processed 45 minutes per pint and 55 minutes per quart.

Review Steps 1 through 12, pages 48–49.

1. Wash the tomatoes, remove decayed spots, core, and stem. Measure the amount needed to fill the jars to be processed in one batch. Scald this number, plus 6 more, ½ minute in a deep pot of boiling water. As you remove each, pull off the skin.

2. Pack the tomatoes into hot jars, leaving ½-inch head room. To each pint jar, add ½ teaspoon of salt; to each quart jar, add 1 full teaspoon of salt. Press the tomatoes gently down into the jars to be sure the jars are firmly packed. Heat the tomato juice to just under boiling, and fill the jars.

3. Follow Steps 9 through 12, pages 48–49. Process pints for 35 minutes, quarts for 45 minutes, at altitudes up to 1,000 feet. (For higher regions, see Altitude Chart, page 48.)

Tomato Juice

Use less perfect tomatoes to make tomato juice, paste, and purée.

Review Steps 1 through 12, pages 48–49.

1. Wash and drain the tomatoes; remove stem ends, core, and any bruises or decayed spots. Cut into small pieces and simmer, without water, over medium heat until well softened, about 5 minutes. Stir often.

2. Press through a food mill or a sieve to remove seeds and skins. Discard this pulp.

3. Reheat sieved juice to the boiling point, add 2 bay leaves, ½ teaspoon oregano, (optional), and salt to taste; do not boil. Strain into hot jars, leaving ¼-inch head room.

4. Follow Steps 9 through 12, pages 48–49. Process pints for 10 minutes, quarts for 15 minutes, at altitudes up to 1,000 feet. (For higher regions, see Altitude Chart, page 48.)

Tomato Paste

Commercial tomato paste is so inexpensive that it is hardly worth making your own, unless you have an oversupply of tomatoes from your garden. It's hard to guess how much paste you'll make from a given quantity of tomatoes, because they differ in meatiness.

However, about 8 quarts of chopped tomatoes will make about 8 half-pints of paste. Can in half-pints only.

Review Steps 1 through 12, pages 48–49.

1. Wash the tomatoes, and stem and core. Place them in a pot and add 1½ cups

OPEN-KETTLE CANNING: Jams, jellies, pickles, relishes, are precooked and then processed in a boiling water bath. Even if your recipes for these foods suggest no processing is necessary, most authorities agree that processing is a guarantee foods will remain wholesome.

seeded sweet peppers, 2 bay leaves, 1 tablespoon salt, and 2 cloves peeled garlic. Cook over medium heat until the tomatoes are soft. Press through a sieve to remove seeds and skins. Discard this pulp.
2. Return the sieved paste to the pan and simmer, uncovered, until it is thick enough to mound on a spoon, about 2½ hours. Stir often to prevent sticking.
3. Pour into hot jars, leaving ¼-inch head room.
4. Follow Steps 9 through 12, pages 48–49. Process half-pints for 45 minutes at altitudes up to 1,000 feet. (For higher regions, see Altitude Chart, page 48.)

Tomato Purée, Seasoned

Use not-so-perfect tomatoes for this purée, but they must be ripe. About 4 quarts of

chopped tomatoes will yield about 8 half-pints of purée. Can only in half-pints.

Review Steps 1 through 12, pages 48–49.

1. Peel, core, and chop 4 quarts of washed tomatoes, and combine with 3 cups of peeled, chopped onions; 1½ cups of seeded, chopped green peppers; and 1 tablespoon of salt. Cook until tender, then press through a sieve.
2. Over medium to low heat, cook purée for 1½ hours, stirring frequently.
3. Pour hot into hot jars, leaving ¼-inch head room.
4. Follow Steps 9 through 12 on pages 48–49. Process half-pints 45 minutes at altitudes of 1,000 feet. (For higher regions, see Altitude Chart, page 48.)

Open-Kettle Canning

Foods canned by the open-kettle method are processed in a boiling water-bath canner, just as are the preceding foods. The difference is that the foods for open-kettle canning are completely precooked before being processed. This is the method used when making baked beans, chili beans, jams, preserves, conserves, and pickled relishes. Making jams, jellies, and pickles is a book in itself, but you can experiment with open-kettle canning procedures by trying the recipes below for mixed relishes.

Recipes for Mixed Vegetable Relish

In all the following recipes, use half-pint jars only. To fill 5 or 6 half-pint jars, you will need: 3 cups finely chopped, scraped carrots; ¾ cup finely chopped, seeded green peppers; ¾ cup finely chopped, seeded red peppers; ¾ cup finely chopped cabbage; ½ cup peeled, finely chopped onion; 2 cups cider vinegar; 1 cup light corn syrup; 1½ tablespoons salt; 1½ teaspoons mustard seed; 1½ teaspoons celery seed.

Review Steps 1 through 12, pages 48–49.

1. In a 6-quart kettle, place the chopped carrots, red and green peppers, cabbage, and onion. Cover with boiling water, and let stand 4 minutes. Drain, and add the vinegar, corn syrup, salt, mustard, and celery seed. Bring to a boil, stirring frequently, then simmer over low heat for 20 minutes, or until the mixture thickens.
2. Pour into hot, half-pint jars, leaving ¼-inch head room.
3. Follow Steps 9 through 12, pages 48–49, and process jars for 10 minutes at altitudes up to 1,000 feet above sea level. (At higher altitudes, see Altitude Chart, page 48.)

Capri Butter

To make 5 half-pint jars, you will need: 2 pounds scraped carrots; ⅛ ounce dried apricots; 1 medium-sized orange, seeded and cut into eighths; 1 cup water; 1 cup light corn syrup; 1 cup sugar; 1 teaspoon ground cinnamon; ¼ teaspoon salt.
Review Steps 1 through 12, pages 48–49.

1. Trim and pare the carrots and cut into 1-inch pieces. Place in a large kettle and add apricots, orange pieces, and water. Cover and bring to a boil over medium heat. Reduce the heat and simmer 15 to 20 minutes, or until the carrots are very tender. Remove from heat and run through a food mill or mash through a sieve
2. Return the purée to the kettle, add corn syrup, sugar, cinnamon, and salt and bring to a boil over medium heat, stirring fre-

quently. Reduce the heat, and simmer for 5 minutes, stirring.
3. Pour into hot jars, leaving ¼-inch head room.
4. Follow Steps 9 through 12, pages 48–49. Process jars for 10 minutes at altitudes up to 1,000 feet. (At higher altitudes, see Altitude Chart, page 48.)

Orange-Beet Conserve

To make 6 half-pint jars, you will need: 9 medium-sized beets, 1 large orange, and 1 medium-sized lemon, cut into eighths and seeded; 2 cups light corn syrup; 2 cups sugar; 1 cup slivered, blanched almonds; 1 tablespoon ground ginger.
Review Steps 1 through 12, pages 48–49.

1. Wash the beets and remove tops; cook in their skins in boiling water 15 minutes, or until tender. Slip off the skins and remove the tap root. Cool the beets and grate coarsely. Slice the orange and lemon pieces very thinly. In a large kettle, mix the beets, orange and lemon slices, corn syrup, and sugar. Bring to a boil over medium heat, stirring constantly. Reduce the heat, and simmer 40 minutes, stirring occasionally. Add the almonds and ginger, mix well, and simmer 5 minutes longer.
2. Pour into hot jars, leaving ¼-inch head room.
3. Follow Steps 9 through 12, on pages 48–49. Process half-pint jars for 5 minutes at altitudes up to 1,000 feet. (For higher regions, see Altitude Chart, page 48.)

Part III
Freezing

6
How to Get the Most from Freezer Foods: Equipment and Supplies

Freezing foods is somewhat easier than canning. However, space for frozen foods is more costly to acquire and maintain than shelf space for canned goods, especially in these days of rising electricity and gas costs.

Should You Buy a Freezer?

Before you purchase a freezer, investigate the possibilities of the freezer compartment in your present refrigerator. Experiment with putting up vegetables and fruits and some of the many convenience foods that the freezer keeps so well; then decide whether you want to get involved with trying to stock a bigger freezer. If a larger freezer isn't used almost to capacity most of the year, you are wasting in maintenance of empty cold space what you may be saving on the items you keep in it.

The amount of freezer space you need depends on the kinds and quantities of foods you intend to store. If freezing is just one of the ways you preserve food, then 3 cubic feet per person is probably adequate. Six cubic feet per person is considered optimum. You can use as much as 10 cubic feet per person if most of the food you preserve is frozen.

Home freezers are available in sizes from less than 3 to more than 30 cubic feet of storage space. If you need more than 10 cubic feet of freezing space—and you have room for it—a separate deep freeze is a good choice. But if your freezer needs are limited and floor space is at a premium (as it is in many apartments and condominiums), then a refrigerator-freezer combination will probably meet your needs best. Refrigerator-freezer combinations which maintain a $-10°F$ temperature will keep foods as long as separate freezer appliances will. Most of the larger refrigerator-freezer combinations contain up to 16 cubic feet and have a separate door for the freezer compartment. The temperature should be kept at $-10°F$ so that when unfrozen food is placed in the freezer, the temperature will stay below $0°F$.

The separate unit upright freezers range in size from 6 to 22 cubic feet and have from three to seven shelves for storing food. The chest freezers range in size from 6 to 8 cubic feet of space.

How Large a Freezer Do I Need?

Before you buy a freezer and start working industriously to fill it, you should know that claims for storing 35 pounds of food per each cubic foot of space aren't absolutely accurate. It may be true in theory, but theories are not the rule in freezers: You can't fill every nook and cranny of the freezer and still manage to find things in it. If you plan to put only square packages into the freezer, you can probably get 32 pounds to a cubic foot. But in my experience, the packages get lumpy and bumpy, especially when you are adding pie shells, breads, coffee cakes, and odd-shaped packages of meats and leftovers. So, to be realistic about it, pare several pounds from advertising claims.

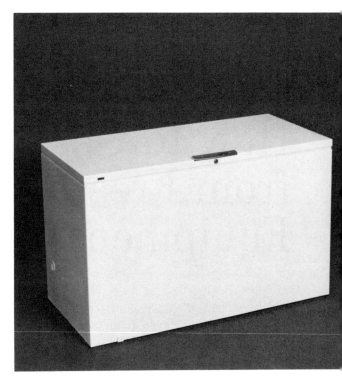

BIG CHEST FREEZER: This large chest freezer with 20.3 cubic feet of storage space holds a lot of frozen food. Look for a model with a signal light that goes on automatically to indicate any power failure.

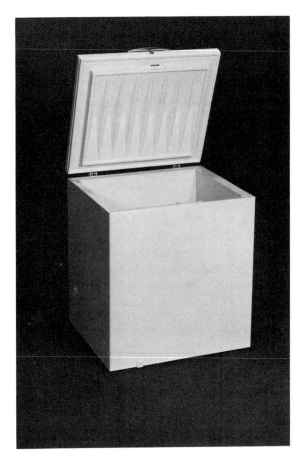

SMALL CHEST FREEZER: The small chest-type freezer (this one holds 5.3 cubic feet) gives plenty of freezing space in an apartment, a vacation home, or anywhere where space is at a premium. It has a sliding basket that holds small items.

The chest-type freezer takes more floor space than the upright and may be hard to maneuver through the house for installation. It also makes foods hard to get at. However, there are those who claim the cold falls out of the upright freezer and that the chest-type maintains the temperature best.

In some chest-type freezers, the coolants are located in the freezer floor and walls. Therefore, unfrozen additions must be placed against the floor or walls, which means you'll have to repack the freezer each time to get the goods to be frozen placed at the coolest spots. Some chest-type freezers have separate fast-freezing compartments. The faster the foods are frozen, the better the texture and flavor.

The upright freezer with shelves makes everything easier to get at. It also takes less floor space, although you will need room enough to open the door. Some uprights have cooling systems in walls and floor, and this presents the problems described above found in some chest freezers. Other uprights have coolants in the shelves as well, and these are preferable.

Look for a freezer with an alarm system that warns you when anything goes wrong with the cooling system or the energy supply. If your freezer doesn't have an alarm, you can buy one for it.

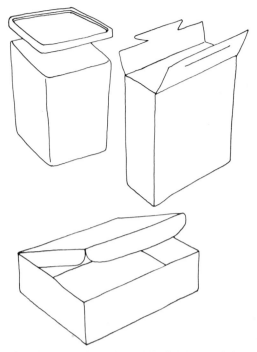

HANDY FREEZER CONTAINERS: Upper left: *plastic box and lid used for foods including liquids.* Upper right: *upright container useful for small lots of foods sealed into plastic bags.* Foreground: *ideal container for packing rows of asparagus, beans, and other vegetables.*

UPRIGHT FREEZER: Advantage of this type of freezer is that it makes food easy to get at and offers a lot of storage space without occupying a lot of floor space. Upright freezers range in size from 6 to 22 cubic feet of storage space. This model holds 19.1 cubic feet.

What Supplies Do I Need?

If you are going to go in for freezing in a big way, in addition to a freezer, you will need proper containers. Frozen foods will only be as good when thawed as the container it was kept in. On the market, you'll find folding cartons with replaceable liners, waxed fiberboard containers, plastic, glass (always allow ½- to ¾-inch head room for foods in glass containers), aluminum baking dishes (which should be well wrapped in freezer paper), and plastic bags of assorted sizes. You'll need heavy freezer paper and freezer tape to close paper-wrapped packages.

When you've used the food in the reusable freezer containers, wash the containers well in very hot, soapy water, and place them with their covers in a storage cabinet. Covers warp in dishwashers—so don't wash them there.

Loading the Freezer

The quantity of food that can be frozen successfully at one time depends on the kind of food and its size, the kind of package, and the design of the freezer. *Put no more unfrozen food into the freezer than will freeze within twenty-four hours.* This is usually 2 to 3 pounds of food per cubic foot of capacity. Overloading slows down the rate of freezing, and foods that freeze slowly may lose their quality or even spoil. Overloading can also raise the temperature above 0°F, which is best for the food already in the freezer.

Try to place each new package in direct contact with the refrigerated surfaces and leave a little space in between. The original flavor, color, and texture, as well as the nutritive value, of frozen foods will be kept intact if the packages are correctly prepared, and if the freezer temperature never goes above 0°F.

What Can I Freeze?

You can freeze almost anything, but not everything will come out tasting as good as it went in. Cake, icing, cream fillings, custards, fried foods, jelly, macaroni, rice, mayonnaise, meringues, potatoes, carrots, and crisply textured vegetables lose quality and appearance when frozen. But almost everything else can be frozen. Cakes, pastries, and breads come out of the freezer a little less moist than they went in. It helps to brush a little water over the tops of breads or pastries before warming.

You can freeze stews successfully, as long as you do not freeze the vegetables. To serve a thawed stew, cook a batch of vegetables and add them, still hot, to the stew before warming.

Thawing Freezer Foods

Do not thaw more frozen food than you intend to use at one time. Once frozen food is thawed, it spoils more rapidly than fresh food. Thaw each package to the desired point by placing it in the refrigerator a few hours

MAKE THAWING EASIER: When filling tall containers, place a double layer of freezer paper every few inches throughout to speed thawing: frozen sections will then separate into small lots that thaw quickly.

(or even overnight) before it is to be used, or set it on a table in a cool room. If you are in a hurry, place the sealed package in *cold* water. (If you thaw it in warm water—and I have when I was desperate—the consistency of the meat or produce may become tough.)

Can Frozen Foods Be Refrozen?

Thawed foods can be refrozen if they are only half-thawed and if there still are ice crystals in the package. Partial thawing may reduce the quality, and if it happens more than once, you'll get a sad-tasting result. Meats and precooked foods may be refrozen if it's certain the temperature did not rise above 32°F.

If you are notified of an impending electricity cut-off and have a freezer full of food, there are some things you can do to prevent thawing. Right away, set the freezer at its top cooling point, and don't open the freezer door until power is resumed. A fully loaded freezer at 0°F will usually stay cool enough, if unopened, to keep foods frozen for a couple of days. If it is only half-loaded, the food may not stay frozen for more than one day.

If the lack of power goes on for more than a day or two, get dry ice to keep the food cool. If you have a lot of food in the freezer, it may be worth your while to haul it to a freezer plant where power is operating. If dry ice is put in the freezer soon after the power goes off, 50 pounds should keep the temperature of food in a 20-cubic foot unit below freezing for three or four days. In a unit with half a load or less, 50 pounds of dry ice will be sufficient for only two or three days.

Work quickly when you put in the dry ice. Place it on thick cardboard, not directly on the packages. *Never touch it with your bare hands.* Make sure the room is well ventilated as you work.

Symptoms of Poor Freezing Practices

Freezer burn is a condition that occurs when food is improperly wrapped. The dry air in the freezer circulates over exposed surfaces, drawing moisture from the food, and causing a dry, stringy surface to develop. Always pack in moisture-resistant packaging, and be sure the package itself is free of air, fully packed, and sealed airtight.

The formation of large ice crystals in foods is the result of slow freezing. When foods are frozen quickly at 0°F or at a lower temperature, the cells in the fiber retain their normal moisture. Slower freezing causes moisture from the fibers to form crystals between the groups of fibers, as a result, the food loses moisture and may darken. Time and temperature have a very important effect on frozen foods. The deterioration of frozen foods speeds up considerably with a rise in the freezer temperature.

How Long Will Frozen Foods Keep?

The table below, prepared by the Ball Corporation, suggests how long the most frequently used foods can be kept frozen without deterioration. Foods will keep longer, especially at temperatures lower than 0°F, but these estimates are a safe guideline.

Frozen Food Storage Periods

Product	Recommended Length of Storage at 0°F
Beef	6–8 months
Bread, Quick (baked)	2 months
Breads, Yeast (baked)	4–8 months
Breads, Yeast (unbaked)	½ month
Butter, Shortenings	5–6 months
Cakes, Unfrosted	6 months
Cakes, Fruit	12 months
Candies, Hard	12 months
Cheese, Cottage	1 month
Cheese (hard or semi-hard)	6–12 months
Cheese (soft)	4 months
Chicken, Poultry	6–9 months
Cookies (baked)	6 months
Cookies (unbaked)	4 months
Eggs	12 months
Fish, Whole, Fillets	2–3 months
Fruits (citrus)	3–4 months
Fruits (non-citrus)	12 months
Game (Rabbit, Squirrel, Opossum)	6–8 months
Gravy	2 months
Ground Meat	3–4 months
Herbs, Raw	8 months
Blanched	10 months
Ice Cream, Sherbet	1–3 months
Jams	12 months
Lamb, Mutton	6–7 months
Liver	3 months
Milk, cream (not sour)	1 month
Onions (uncooked)	3–6 months
Opossum, Rabbit; Squirrel	6–8 months
Pastry (unbaked)	2 months
Pies (baked)	1 month
Pies (unbaked)	3 months
Pizza	1 month
Pork (cured)	1–2 months
Pork (fresh)	3–4 months
Pork	3–4 months
Prepared Main Dishes	3–6 months
Salads	2 months
Sandwiches	1 month
Sausage	4–6 months
Shellfish, Except Shrimp	3–4 months
Shrimp	6 months
Soups, Stews	6 months
Turkey	6 months
Veal	3–4 months
Vegetables (cooked)	1 month
Vegetables (blanched, except Onions)	12 months
Venison	6–8 months

How Do I Freeze What?

Meats for freezing must be wrapped correctly, and the packages sealed properly if they are to remain at their prime during freezing. Some fruits can be sugared and frozen, while others must be frozen in a syrup. Vegetables are usually blanched (scalded), before freezing. Prepared foods are completely cooked, then carefully wrapped, and frozen. The following chapters will show you the five basic methods of preparing meats and foods for freezing and give you recipes for the method that is best for the food you want to freeze.

7
Buying and Wrapping Foods for the Freezer

Because meat takes a big chunk of the food dollar, it deserves the most freezer space. Can you save money by buying a side of beef, pork, or lamb? You can best answer the question yourself by pricing a whole carcass, a side, or a quarter, and wholesale cuts at a local meat wholesaler.

Buying Meats for Freezing

A carcass side, or a quarter carcass, is sold by its "hanging weight," the weight before being cut into chops, roasts, and so on. For a beef carcass, losses in cutting vary from 20 to 30 percent, or more. Take this into consideration when toting up the advantages and disadvantages of the price per carcass.

You also need to know the yield grade of meats when buying in such quantities. Yield Grade I is the highest, and Grade V the lowest. Grade I means the carcass will yield 79.8 percent or more in retail cuts; Grade V yields 65.9 percent.

In whatever quantity you buy beef, take special note of the quality. Beef varies more in quality than other meats. The most widely sold grade is USDA Choice. USDA Prime is the best.

In buying fowl, chicken, duck, or turkey, consider whether they have been frozen before and thawed. They can be refrozen, but they'll be of better quality if they are available "fresh killed." Take advantage of buys in cut-up poultry.

Packaging Is the Key to Success

The only really suitable wrapping paper for freezer foods is the wrapping paper sold expressly for this purpose. Moisture- and vapor-proof materials especially designed to wrap foods for freezing are resistant to grease and oil and are liquid and stainproof. They are sturdy and stick tightly to the surfaces of the foods, but lift off easily. Ordinary waxed papers are not adequate protection.

There are several types of bags and boxes and round containers available made of such materials. Moisture- and vapor-proof plastic films, cellophane, polyethylene, Saran-type wraps, and foils are sold in freezer weights. There are laminated papers as well. Heavily waxed freezer paper is most often used. Freezer tapes for sealing plastic packaging are also offered. Glass freezer jars are good for sauces and preserves.

Step-by-Step Procedure for Buying and Wrapping Foods

Step 1: Select prime, or choice, grades of meat and buy cuts suited to family use. Have excess fat and bone removed.

Step 2: Keep meats stored in refrigerator at 40°F if they must wait for processing. Keep all cuts cool in the refrigerator as you process the first pieces.

Step 3: Trim away any remaining excess fat or bone. Wrap protruding bone ends in foil padding to avoid piercing wrapping paper.

Step 4: Group the steaks, chops, or fillets into family portions, and separate each piece or fillet with moisture-proof paper. Wrap in freezer paper, film, or foil. Make sure the paper adheres to all surfaces, shutting out any air. Tape firmly closed with freezer tape. Overwrap with a second thickness of film and seal with heated hand iron, or tape shut. Wrap roasts and ground meats as above.

Step 5: As each piece is wrapped, place it in the freezer on the surface that contains the freezing coils. Reposition already frozen foods to make room for the newly added food to ensure that the new food is in contact with the freezing surfaces of the compartment.

If You Are Packing Bags, Boxes, or Jars

Wrapped foods rarely hold air in the packages, but bagged foods often do. To make sure bagged foods contain no air, press out as much air as possible, molding the bag to the shape of the food. Then twist the top of the bag, double it over and close with ties or string. When storing in boxes, cartons, or glass jars,

line the container with a plastic storage bag, draw the air from the bag, use a tie to seal it closed, then close the container. Leave ½- to 1-inch head space in glass containers.

PREPARING MEATS FOR FREEZING: A fast and easy way to wrap ground meat, chops, and steaks for freezing is to lay them on a double thickness of freezer film, cut the film into squares around them, then pile the meats on their squares together in portions large enough for one family meal.

PACK IN FAMILY-SIZE LOTS: Put together in one freezer bundle only as much meat as you will serve at one meal. Label each package with the number of portions included and the date of packing.

Preparing
Meats for Freezing

Meats: Beef, lamb, mutton, and veal, in roasts, rolled roasts, steaks, chops, stew meat, and frying meat may be stored frozen for one year, but will be best if used within the period indicated on page 63. Liver should not be stored more than three months. Pork should not be stored longer than six months. Three to four months is considered the longest period ground meat should be stored frozen.

If you buy a side or quarter, buy only good quality carcasses that have been aged one week. Trim away as much fat and bone as you can. Wrap bones that protrude in a wad of foil before wrapping in freezer paper, otherwise the bones may pierce the wrapping paper.

Wrap large roasts individually in freezer film, foil, or paper. Wrap steaks and chops the same way, but use a double layer of moisture-proof material between each piece to make it easier to separate and thaw the individual pieces. Wrap ground meat in family-sized portions.

Game Meats: Small animals, such as rabbit and squirrel, if well cleaned when they are killed, keep well when frozen. They should be used within six months. Skin, wrap, and seal into foil or film as described for beef. Clean, pluck, and prepare game birds as poultry.

Poultry: For short storage, wrap plucked, cleaned whole birds in freezer film and overwrap with freezer paper. Remember, the livers won't keep more than three months, so wrap separately and label carefully. You can wrap and freeze the fleshy pieces, with a double layer of moisture-proof material between pieces to make thawing faster and easier. Cook the bony parts, wings, back, and necks, remove the meat, and freeze it. The recommended storage time for cooked poultry is *shorter* than the time for uncooked poultry. Then overwrap the whole packages in freezer film, with freezer paper over it.

Handling
Seafood for Freezing

Fish: Fish freezes well, and is excellent if it is really fresh when frozen. Clean small fish, scale them, and freeze them whole, separated by moisture-proof material. If the catch is large, fillet the fish before freezing. To fillet, slide a very sharp knife sideways along the dorsal bone and under the thickest portion of the flesh. Cut the flesh off the bones in a single piece. Wrap and freeze filleted fish in portions suitable for two persons. Big fish, such as swordfish and large salmon, can be cut crosswise into steaks. Dip steaks and fillets 30 seconds in a solution of ⅔ cup salt to 1 gallon of water, then wrap each piece tightly in freezer film, and overwrap with freezer paper.

Shrimp: Fresh-caught shrimp, if small, should have just the heads removed before freezing in bunches in plastic freezer bags. For larger shrimp, remove the heads, shell the shrimp, remove the vein down the back, then freeze. If you want to cook the shrimp before freezing, clean it, plunge unshelled into rapidly boiling water containing 1 peeled onion, 1 bay leaf, ¼ teaspoon thyme, 1 tablespoon salt; bring the water back to a boil, and simmer, uncovered, five minutes; then drain, and pack into freezer bags.

Preparing Dairy
Products for Freezing

Eggs: Whole eggs, as well as yolks and whites, can be frozen, but the uses for them after thawing are limited to baking or scrambling. Break *whole* eggs and force through a sieve, then package in quantities you are likely to use at one time in small plastic storage bags, seal and place the bags in layers in a freezer jar or plastic box with a close-fitting lid. *Whites* can be frozen in the same manner. *Yolks* can be frozen in the same manner, but add ½ teaspoon of salt for each 6 yolks, to reduce coagulation.

Milk and Cream: Store milk in freezer cans or plastic freezer cartons leaving a 2-inch head space. Freeze only heavy cream containing 40 percent, or more, butterfat. Heat to 180° for 15 minutes, adding ½ teaspoon sugar before freezing. Better yet, whip heavy cream with sugar, before freezing; it comes out rather well. Package first in plastic storage bags, then place bags in plastic freezer boxes or cartons. Or, if cream is very fresh, freeze in its container, and whip after removing when still very cold. Remember to leave head space, so the liquids can expand as they freeze without destroying the container.

Butter: Good quality, really fresh butter, margarine, or shortening freezes well. Wrap tightly, to seal air out, in freezer film, then place the blocks in freezer bags, cartons, or plastic boxes.

Cheese: Cut hard or semi-hard cheese in ½-pound or 1-pound pieces, wrap tightly in freezer film, overwrap in heavy freezer paper, and seal with freezer tape. Wrap soft cheese in freezer bags, draw out all the air until the sides of the bag cling to the cheese. Next, seal, then place in plastic freezer boxes or cartons, and freeze.

None of these products, except butter, is quite the same after freezing, but freezing is a good way to store them if you have a large supply on hand and are leaving town.

8
Vegetables and the Blanching Method: Recipes

To "blanch" vegetables simply means to scald them by immersing them briefly in rapidly boiling water. Most vegetables meant for freezing must first be blanched, but a few, green peppers, onions, and the herbs, do not require real blanching, and are simply scalded for freezing. Other vegetables, such as pumpkin and winter squashes, are completely cooked before freezing.

Improper wrapping is the major cause for disappointment encountered in home freezing. The most available, and the most popular, freezer packages are described on pages 61 and 65–66.

What About Improvised Containers?

Some make sense, and some don't. Waxed containers, such as milk cartons, will crack at 0°F. Coffee cans with plastic lids are great, but you must first line the interior of the can with freezer film or bags, then suck the air from the bag or film and use a twist or a heated iron to seal tightly before closing the can.

Glass jars of all sorts, as long as they have close-fitting tops, are excellent, but you must be sure to leave enough head room for the contents to expand. One drawback of the glass container is that it is hard to get the contents out for thawing, and in the jar they tend to thaw slowly.

DOUBLE PACKAGING FOR SMALL LOTS: Pack meal-size portions of small fruits and vegetables into small plastic storage bags, then store several bags in one freezer container. This saves space, and gives foods double protection from the drying air of the freezer.

Plastic bags of all kinds make excellent freezer containers. However, the thin-filmed ones should be overwrapped by something else because thin film doesn't create enough of a barrier to protect the moisture inside from the dehydrating influence of the freezer, as long as you are freezing a large enough quantity to warrant a very large container. Draw all the air from the bag before sealing it.

When using any plastic bag for freezing, beware of puncturing it. Use a twist to tie it shut. (You will also find twists most useful for packages whose content is frequently being used—for instance, herbs, green pepper slices, or onion slices.)

When you are improvising storage containers, it is important to consider whether or not it will be easy to remove the contents from these containers when frozen, and whether or not such containers will cause packing problems in the freezer. Straight-sided containers (square or round) stack most easily and use freezer space most efficiently.

Freeze portions to be used by your family at one meal. The size of the containers to be used depends on the number of servings needed. A pint package will usually serve three to four persons.

Labeling

Don't forget to label packages with their contents, the date they were frozen, and how many portions they contain. If you have space, you might add a note about where the food came from, because it's fun to see how Aunt Sally's broccoli turned out.

Equipment for Blanching

The only special equipment you'll need for blanching—and you may have it already—is a wire basket to hold the vegetables while they are in the blanching water. You can use a double layer of cheesecloth folded to create a bag but it's less practical than a wire basket. You can also use a wire colander; but if you do, add a few seconds to the blanching time, for it will take a moment longer to heat up once immersed in the water.

Step-by-Step Blanching Procedures for Vegetables and Herbs

Whether you're blanching a vegetable that requires 4 minutes, or an herb that takes 30 seconds, the procedures are the same. Have your equipment and packages ready before you begin. Label the packages before filling.

Step 1: You can comfortably blanch only 4 cups of prepared vegetables at once, so work out how much produce you need to make 4 cups. Keep the rest stored in the refrigerator until it's time to use it.

Step 2: Remove foliage if any, wash the vegetables, and cut out any damaged or bruised parts. Prepare as you would for cooking by chopping, slicing, or quartering.

Step 3: While you are preparing the vegetables, bring 4 quarts of water to a full boil in a

very large kettle. Fill the sink with cold water and add half the cubes of an ice cube tray before you start blanching.

Step 4: Place 4 cups of prepared vegetables in a wire basket, and plunge them into the boiling water. Cover the kettle at once, leave the heat high, and *immediately* start counting out the blanching time required in each recipe.

Step 5: At the moment the blanching time is up, remove the basket from the boiling water, and plunge it into the ice water in the sink. Cool it there for exactly the same period as for blanching. Remove, and drain the vegetables.

Step 6: Fill packages fully to exclude as much air as possible. Close, seal, and place at once in the freezer directly on the refrigerator surface or in the fast-freezing compartment, if you have one. When you place the packages in the freezer, leave some space between them, if possible.

Hints and Tips

If you are going to do a lot of blanching, you will need a lot of ice, so the night before fill as many bread loaf pans and other containers of similar size as you can with water, and freeze. You can use the blanching water for 8 loads before changing it.

Any vegetables that seem less than perfect, set aside and use fresh. Don't waste time freezing them—they will be inferior.

Recipes

Artichokes

In some areas, especially in California, artichokes can be purchased at bargain prices. Buy the smallest sizes you can find.

Review Steps 1 through 6, pages 70–71.

1. Wash the artichoke well. Remove and discard the outer leaves until you come to rather soft, inner leaves. Slice the vegetable through the center, lengthwise.
2. Blanch in boiling water 3 minutes for small artichokes, 4 minutes for larger artichokes.

BLANCHING VEGETABLES FOR FREEZING: *Neat blanching unit consists of a tall, narrow kettle fitted with a blanching basket. Blanching preserves flavor, texture, and color by retarding action of the enzymes that ripen food.*

COOLING BLANCHED VEGETABLES: *Blanched vegetables are quick-cooled by placing them in a sink filled with water and ice. Cool for exactly the same length of time food was blanched.*

3. Cool, drain upside down on paper towels until all the water is gone.
4. Squeeze tightly together in containers. Seal, freeze.

Asparagus

Review Steps 1 through 6, pages 70–71.

1. Sort spears according to thickness for freezing and prepare as for canning, page 40. Cut into lengths suited to the size of your freezer package, usually 5 to 6 inches long. (If you have leftover green ends that are tender, save these and make soup with them.)
2. Blanch each size group in boiling water, 2 minutes for very thin spears, 3 minutes for medium ones, and 4 minutes for thick ones.
3. Cool; drain; lay neatly in containers for freezing. Mix sizes in each package if you like.

Beans: Lima

Review Steps 1 through 6, pages 70–71.

1. Wash and shell the beans. If you have trouble breaking the pods open, plunge them into boiling water for ½ minute, cool, then pull down hard on the string. Sort the shelled beans according to size.
2. Blanch larger beans 4 minutes, medium beans 3 minutes, small beans 2 minutes.
3. Cool; drain; pack beans loosely into containers, but fill containers to the tops.

Beans: Green, Snap, Wax

Select pencil-slim beans, 6 to 8 inches long and very fresh.
Review Steps 1 through 6, pages 70–71.

1. Wash the beans, snip off ends, sort according to length and thickness, and plan to blanch similar sizes in batches. Beans may be frozen whole or cut into 1- to 1½-inch pieces. Very thick beans may be Frenched —sliced in half through the middle.
2. Blanch whole beans 3 minutes, cut beans 2 minutes, Frenched beans 1 minute.
3. Cool; drain on towels; pack and freeze.

Broccoli

Select only small young shoots with stems not more than 1 inch thick. If you can't find broccoli this size, select fresh, larger heads; use a potato peeler to remove the outer skin of the stems; and cut the heads into spears with stems 1-inch thick.
Review Steps 1 through 6 on pages 70–71.

1. Soak the broccoli in a salt solution (1 teaspoon salt to each quart of water) for 1 hour, then rinse in two changes of water. Cut the broccoli to uniform spears.
2. Blanch 3 minutes for thicker heads, 2 minutes for thin heads.
3. Cool; drain on towels; pack carefully aligned and freeze in containers.

Brussels Sprouts

Select only small, dark green sprouts for freezing.
Review Steps 1 through 6 on pages 70–71.

1. Soak the sprouts in a salt solution (1 teaspoon salt to each quart) for 1 hour; rinse well in cold water.
2. Blanch large sprouts 5 minutes, medium sprouts 4 minutes, small sprouts 3 minutes.
3. Cool; drain well; pack and freeze.

Cauliflower

Select tightly curled, pure white heads for freezing.
Review Steps 1 through 6 on pages 70–71.

1. Break the heads into small florets of uniform size, and discard the large stem ends. Soak in a salt solution (1 teaspoon salt to each quart of water) for 1 hour, then rinse well in several changes of cold water.
2. Add to the boiling blanching water the juice of two lemons to keep the florets white. Blanch pieces larger than 1 inch for 4 minutes; 1-inch or smaller pieces for 3 minutes.
3. Cool; drain on toweling; pack and freeze.

Chard

Select tightly curled leaves on crisp, fresh stems.

Gourmets treat the stems like asparagus, and sometimes stuff it.

Review Steps 1 through 6 on pages 70–71.

1. Tear uniform-sized pieces of leaves from the stems, and wash them well in several changes of water.
2. Pack closely into a wire basket and blanch exactly 1 minute.
3. Plunge into cold wash, swish once or twice, drain, and press out as much water as you can. Pack, pressed firmly into containers, and freeze.

Collard Greens

Prepare and freeze collard greens as described for Chard in the preceding recipe. Be sure you get as much water as possible out of the greens before packaging.

Corn: Whole Ears

Frozen young, just-picked ears of corn after blanching seem to taste almost as good as when just picked. Less perfect ears should be put up as whole kernels.

Freeze corn as soon after picking as possible (within a half hour).

Review Steps 1 through 6 on pages 70–71.

1. While the water is heating, husk the ears, wash quickly under running water to remove silk. Set aside any imperfect or too large ears.
2. Blanch 7 minutes for large ears, 5 minutes for medium ears, and 4 minutes for small ears.
3. Cool, drain quickly, dry with paper towel, and pack similar sizes together in each package. Freeze.

Corn: Kernels

Review Steps 1 through 6 on pages 70–71.

1. Husk and wash corn, making sure all silk is gone.
2. Blanch long enough to cook the kernels, about 10 minutes for large ears if they are really fresh.
3. Cool, drain, and dry corn. With a sharp knife, slice the kernels from the cob as close as you can get without getting bits of cob in the mixture. Package at once, and freeze.

Green Onions

You can put these up in large bags, close with a twist, and use as needed. They'll be limp but flavorful when thawed.

Review Steps 1 through 6 on pages 70–71.

1. Clean the onions, slice off root ends and toughest portion of stalks. Remove outer skin. Chop with a knife or a food chopper.
2. Place in a large plastic freezer bag, suck out the air, and close with a twist tie. Freeze.

Herbs

All tender herbs may be frozen. When thawed they are too limp to use in salads, but have excellent flavor for cooking.

1. Pick parsley, basil, dill, tarragon, chives, or thyme in the early morning before the heat of the sun draws the moisture from them. Wash quickly under a spray, and break into sprigs.
2. Wrap in cheesecloth bundles, and blanch 30 seconds.

3. Plunge into ice water, drain, unwrap, and drop herbs onto paper towel. Pat dry. Pack in plastic bags, sealed with twists. Freeze. To use, untie the twists, remove a few sprigs, seal the bag, and return to the freezer.

Kale

Freeze only very fresh, crisp, curly leaves. Review Steps 1 through 6 on pages 70–71.

1. Tear leaves into bits, and wash thoroughly in several changes of water.
2. Pack closely into wire basket, and blanch 1 minute.
3. Plunge into cold wash, swish through once or twice, drain. Press water from the basket with your hand. Pack, pressed firmly into containers, and freeze.

Okra

Freeze only very small, young, tender, fresh pods.
Review Steps 1 through 6 on pages 70–71.

1. Wash well, and sort into uniform sizes.
2. Blanch large pods 3 minutes, medium pods 2 minutes, very small pods 1 minute.
3. Cool in ice water, drain, dry, cut off stem end. If you wish, slice pods into slices ½-inch thick for freezing. Pack, freeze.

Onions: Chopped

Chopped onions may be frozen as described for Green Onions. You may find it a shortcut to chop the onions by running thick slices, a few at a time, through the blender at low speed. Bag the onions and use as needed.

Onions: Whole

Frozen small, white onions are excellent for making creamed onions, among other uses.
Review Steps 1 through 6 on pages 70–71.

1. Peel the onions, and grade according to size. Plan to blanch in batches of similar sizes.

2. Place the onions in cheesecloth bags one group at a time. Blanch small onions 3 minutes, medium onions 5 minutes, large onions 7 minutes.
3. Cool, drain well. Pack and freeze.

Peas: Green

Only very small, tender peas will be good frozen, so not every bargain in spring peas is really worth investing in for freezing.
Review Steps 1 through 6 on pages 70–71.

1. Wash the pods, and shell the peas. Grade according to size, and plan to blanch only similar sizes together. Overcooking will spoil them.
2. Blanch 1 minute for tiny peas, 2 minutes for larger sizes.
3. Cool, drain, dry on paper towel, pack and freeze.

Peas with Onions

Review Steps 1 through 6 on pages 70–71.

1. Wash and sort peas as described in the preceding recipe.
2. Blanch tiny white onions (preferably less than 1-inch round) or the white heads of large green onions for 2 minutes.
3. Add the peas to the onions and blanch 1 minute more with the onions. Cool, drain, and pack peas and onions together, taking care to distribute onions evenly among the packages.

Peppers: Green

Select fully mature peppers, thick-fleshed, and shiny-skinned, for freezing. Package rings, strips, and pieces in large plastic bags tied at the mouth with twists. Then, when needed, you can take out a few rings or chips without thawing the whole container.
Review Steps 1 through 6 on pages 70–71.

1. Peppers do not have to be blanched and can be frozen whole or cut. Wash the peppers, cut out the stem ends, use a spoon to scoop out all the seeds, then rinse well to float away any remaining seeds. Leave whole, or

cut into halves, quarters, long strips, 2-inch chunks, or into round rings.

2. If you *want* to blanch them so they will be precooked, blanch whole peppers 4 minutes; half peppers 3 minutes; rings, pieces, and strips 2 minutes.
3. Cool, drain, dry well; pack and freeze.

Pumpkin

Use this recipe to make pies or to serve as a vegetable. It tastes rather like summer squash. Simmer thawed pumpkin until all the liquid is gone. If using as a vegetable, butter well, and add salt and plenty of pepper before serving. You can pack this in 2-cup lots, the amount many pumpkin pie recipes call for.
Review Steps 1 through 6 on pages 70–71.

1. Peel the pumpkin, remove the seeds and stringy parts, and cut into 2-inch chunks. In an ordinary kettle, boil the pieces until tender, 10 minutes or more.
2. With a potato masher, mash to a fine purée. Cool in the kettle, stirring to hasten the process.
3. Pack into containers, leaving ½-inch head space.

Spinach

Select only very young, very crisp, tender leaves for freezing. Avoid spinach that has thick stems, and don't buy packages of spinach with the roots still attached.
Review Steps 1 through 6 on pages 70–71.

1. Remove tough stalks, and wash the spinach in six or seven changes of water, or until a bowlful of the spinach soaked in water leaves no trace whatsoever of sand in the bottom of the container when the spinach is lifted out.
2. Pack firmly into scalding basket, and blanch exactly 1 minute.
3. Cool by swishing several times in ice water; drain, squeeze out as much water as possible; press firmly into containers and freeze.

Squash: Summer, Zucchini, Marrow

Select only vegetables 5 to 8 inches long, slim, and with very shiny skins so thin you can break them with your fingernail.
Review Steps 1 through 6 on pages 70–71.

1. Wash the vegetables, remove stem ends, and slice into rounds ¼ inch thick. Do not peel.
2. Blanch for 3 minutes.
3. Cool, drain, pack and freeze.

Squash: Winter

Prepare as in the recipe for Pumpkin on this page. Winter squash contains much less moisture than pumpkin and won't require the drying time recommended for pumpkin. Leave ½-inch head space when packing in containers.

Succotash

This is a mixture of two-thirds whole-kernel corn and one-third lima beans.
Review Steps 1 through 6 on pages 70–71.

1. Prepare and blanch corn kernels as directed on page 73.
2. Prepare and blanch lima beans as directed on page 72.
3. Cool kernels and lima beans; mix together. Package and freeze.

Tomatoes: Whole

Tomatoes can be frozen raw and unblanched, but the texture is spoiled by the freezing and they aren't really good for salads. For freezing, select small, meaty tomatoes that are completely ripe, without bruises or blemishes.
Review Steps 1 through 6 on pages 70–71.

1. Wash, stem, and core the tomatoes.
2. Blanch in boiling water 30 seconds, dip in cool water, and peel away the skins.

3. Place in a large kettle over medium heat, heat until juices flow, and simmer until soft, about 5 minutes.
4. Cool by placing the kettle in a sinkful of ice water.
5. Pack tomatoes and juice, evenly distributed, into upright containers. To fill containers, add tomato juice if you like. Freeze.

Tomatoes: Green

With the first threat of frost, often there is a healthy crop of tomatoes in all stages—half ripe, large, and green, down to immature.

These are wonderful in many Italian dishes or when cooked with eggs or when served as a cooked vegetable with butter, salt, pepper, and oregano.

1. Wash, core, stem the tomatoes, and slice into rounds ¼ inch thick.
2. Place freezer squares between each round.
3. Seal in plastic bags, place in freezer container, and freeze.

9
Two Methods for Preparing Fruit: Recipes

Fruits freeze well, though not all retain crisp textures under freezing. Berries, which freeze well whole, can be sprinkled with sugar and packed without further preparation. Apple slices for use in pies can be blanched and frozen. Most other fruits are packed in syrups, though some are blanched or cooked first.

Packaging for Fruits

Because many of the fruits are packed in syrup, they should be stored in containers that won't leak. Plastic boxes and freeze jars, straight-sided, without shoulders are my preferences. On occasion, you can improvise and pack fruits in containers like coffee cans with plastic liners.

Fill the containers full so there are no air pockets, or as few as possible, when packing fruits dry. When packing fruits with syrups, fill the containers, leaving about ½-inch head room in quart containers, ¼-inch head room in pint containers.

Preventing Discoloration in Fruits

Because some acid is present in most fruits, they may discolor if they come into contact with iron. Make sure knives, mixing bowls, pans and other utensils are enameled or made of stainless steel, or of other non-corrosive material.

Peaches, apples, and pears, and some other fruits as well, darken when cut surfaces are exposed to the air. To prevent this discoloration, drop each piece as it is cut into an ascorbic acid solution. (See page 49.)

How Much Do I Package? What Size Container?

Package only as much fruit in one container as you are likely to use at one meal, or to make one pie. One quart of berries will give you generous portions for four as dessert; a pint of applesauce will serve the same number of people. If you are freezing fruit for pie-making, a quart of fruit is as much as you can use in a 9-inch pie.

Three Ways to Pack Fruit for Freezing

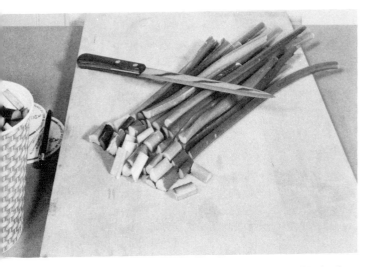

DRY-PACKING FOR THE FREEZER: Rhubarb stalks cut into even lengths are packed into freezer container, sealed, and frozen. This method is suitable for whole, ripe berries, fruit slices, and sweet pepper strips.

Dry-Pack, Unsweetened: Whole, fresh berries and fruits that will be made into pies can be packed dry, without sugar. You can pack and freeze fruits intended for preserves this way, too, if you get caught with fruit you mean to jam and don't have time. It's also a good way to freeze fruits if members of your family are on no-sugar diets.

Here's the step-by-step method:

1. Pick over, discard bruised or imperfect fruit, or portions of fruit. Hull the fruit; or peel, slice, or quarter; or leave whole.
2. Wash quickly in ice water; don't let the fruit get water-logged.
3. Drain, spread on paper towels to dry. Pat dry fruit that seems especially wet.
4. Pour from towels into containers, allowing ½- to ¼-inch head room. Seal, and freeze at once. Freeze each package as it is ready.

Remember to label containers before you start.

Dry-Pack, Sweetened: Whole, fresh berries and fruits to be made into pies and compotes

FIRMING SMALL SOFT FRUITS: Firm small, soft fruits before freezing dry or sugar-packing by soaking them in ice water. This cleans the berries and allows you to sort out bruised or spoiled fruit while the rest of the fruit is firming.

DRY-PACKING WITH SUGAR: Sliced berries, whole berries, and pieces of peeled fruit may be sugared, as shown here, then packed into freezer containers without further processing.

can also be packed dry, with sugar. Fruits which darken after peeling and cutting, are packed in a mixture of citric acid and sugar, 3 teaspoons of ascorbic-citric acid to each 2 cups of sugar.

Here's the step-by-step method:

1. Pick over, discard bruised or imperfect fruit, or pieces of fruit. Hull the fruit; or peel, slice, or quarter; or leave whole.
2. Wash quickly in ice water. It helps firm the flesh of the fruit.
3. Drain; spread on paper towels to dry.
4. Sprinkle sugar, or acid and sugar mixture, on the bottom of the container and pack in one-quarter of the fruit; sprinkle sugar or acid and sugar mixture over the fruit. Repeat three times until the container is full, and top with a layer of sugar or acid-sugar mixture. Seal and label. Freeze.

Syrup-Packed Fruit: This is the method used with most fruits. It is used with berries that have little juice or a pale flavor, for fruits that change color quickly when exposed to air, and for fruits to be served as compotes or in syrup. These fruits won't retain their full texture except for the berries and melon balls. For that reason, you may prefer (as I do) to can fruits you want to serve in syrup or to mix into fruit salads. The texture of the canned fruit is better.

You can make syrup with plain water, or, if you have it, with fruit juice. To make a sugar syrup, add the sugar to just-boiling water, stir until the sugar is dissolved, then chill.

Sugar Syrups for Freezing Fruit

Type of Syrup	Amount of Sugar	Amount of Water	Yield in Syrup
20 percent	1 cup	4 cups	5 cups
30 percent	2 cups	4 cups	5⅓ cups
40 percent	3 cups	4 cups	5½ cups
50 percent	4¾ cups	4 cups	6½ cups
60 percent	7 cups	4 cups	7¾ cups

A 20 percent syrup is a *light syrup*, 30 percent a *medium syrup*, 40 percent a *medium*

FRUIT PACKED WITH SYRUP: *Syrup solution is poured into a freezer jar, which is then packed with prepared and processed fruit slices. Push slices down into the syrup with a bunched wad of plastic film. Or, an alternate method is to pack fruit into jars, then cover with boiling syrup.*

heavy syrup, 50 percent a *heavy syrup*, 60 percent an *extra heavy syrup*.

If you wish to use a mixture of granulated sugar with corn syrup to make your packing syrup, mix these proportions: *light syrup*, 1 cup sugar, to 2 cups corn syrup, to 6 cups water—yield, 8 cups syrup; *medium syrup*, 2 cups sugar, to 2 cups corn syrup, to 5 cups water—yield, 8 cups syrup; *heavy syrup*, 3 cups sugar, to 2 cups corn syrup, to 4 cups water—yield, 8 cups syrup. Make these syrups with cold water, then chill.

If you are strongly in favor of honey, you can substitute honey for corn syrup, but be wary: honey as a distinct flavor of its own which may overpower the flavor of the fruit.

When adding ascorbic acid to syrups to prevent the darkening of fruits, add it to the syrup after it has chilled in the refrigerator, and mix well.

How Long Will It Keep?

Properly prepared and packaged fruits will keep up to 1 year at 0°F. However, precooked fruits, such as applesauce, should be used within 4 months.

In the following recipes, work with no more than 4 cups of fruit at one time.

Recipes

Apples: Slices

1. Bring 4 quarts of water to a rapid boil while you are preparing the apples.
2. Wash, core and peel the apples, cut into ¼-inch rounds and drop into an ascorbic-citric mixture of 2 tablespoons of acid to 1 gallon of cold water.
3. Rinse the apple slices well, and place in a cheesecloth bag or in an enameled colander.
4. Place the colander or cheesecloth bag in the boiling water and blanch apple slices for 2 minutes. (See Chapter 8.)
5. Cool in a sinkful of ice water, 2 minutes.
6. Drain, dry on paper towel, and pack in freezer containers or in large, freezer-weight plastic bags. Seal. Freeze.

Apricots

1. Bring 4 quarts of water to a rapid boil while you are preparing the fruit.
2. Wash apricots well, cut into halves, remove the pits. Peeling is optional.
3. Place the apricots in an enameled colander, and blanch in the boiling water for ½ minute.
4. Chill in ice water. Drain and dry.
5. Pack in freezer containers, and fill the containers with a 40 percent fruit syrup, leaving ½-inch head room. Freeze.

Apricot Slices for Pies

Prepare the apricots as in preceding recipe, but peel before cutting into ¼-inch thick rounds. Drop into boiling water for 1 minute. Chill, dry, and pack in large plastic bags. Tie bags tightly with twists. When frozen, you can remove as many slices as needed to make pies, and then reclose the bag.

Blackberries

1. Hull, rinse quickly in ice water, and drain. Dry well.
2. Pack without sugar, loosely, into rigid containers. Seal. Freeze.

Blueberries

1. Sort carefully, discarding bruised or damaged berries. Wash in ice water, drain, and dry on paper towel.
2. Pack loosely, without sugar, into rigid containers. Seal. Freeze. Or pack with sugar, using ½ cup sugar to every 4 cups of berries. Toss the berries with the sugar before packaging.

Cherries: Sour

Freeze only ripe cherries with good color. If you want to freeze these pitted, you can buy one of those pitting gadgets offered by hardware shops.

1. Drop the cherries into ice water to firm the fruit, and leave them there for 1 hour. Pit and stem the cherries.
2. Drain, dry well, and toss with sugar, using 1½ cups of sugar to every 4 quarts of cherries. Pack into freezer containers, leaving ½ inch of head room. Seal. Freeze.

Cherries: Sweet

Freeze only very good quality fruit.

1. Wash and stem the cherries. Don't try to pit sweet cherries. Drain and dry well.
2. Spread the cherries out on the fast-freeze compartment of the freezer, or on refrigerated surface near the coolants.
3. When the cherries are frozen hard, bag them, tie the bag with a twist, and store in the freezer.

Cranberries

Wash, dry, and freeze cranberries as in the preceding recipe for Sweet Cherries.

Melon Balls

Really ripe, fully-flavored cantaloupes and honey dew melons are excellent prepared this way. They are even better if you sprinkle the melon balls with 1 tablespoon of Cointreau liqueur and let them soak in it for 20 minutes before freezing.

1. Halve the melons, remove the seeds, scrape out all pulp, and peel carefully so that all the hard green flesh close to the rind is removed.
2. Use a melon scoop or a round teaspoon to scoop balls from each melon half. (Use the remaining pieces of melon to make fresh fruit salad, for immediate use.)
3. Pack the half-and-half mixture of cantaloupe and honey dew balls, or the all-cantaloupe or all honey-dew melon balls, into pint-size plastic bags. Sprinkle with 1 teaspoon lemon juice, strained, and/or 2 teaspoons sugar. Seal the bags with twists, shake them a little to spread the juice and/or sugar. Pack the bags into freezer boxes. Freeze.

Peaches

1. Prepare a solution of 2 tablespoons of ascorbic-citric acid to 1 gallon of ice water.
2. Peel peaches under cold running water, pit them, and slice them into the ascorbic-citric acid solution. Prepare 8 cups.
3. Fill freezer containers ¼ full with a 40 percent syrup.
4. Remove peaches from the ascorbic-citric acid solution, and pack into containers. Leave ½-inch head room. Cover. Freeze.

Raspberries

1. Sort berries carefully, using only the firm large berries. (Use the soft specimens for a puréed dessert, fresh.)
2. Plunge the berries into ice water, using a colander to hold them. Drain, and dry well on paper towel.
3. Pack with sugar, about ⅔ cups of sugar to each quart of berries, as described on pages 78–79. Freeze.

Rhubarb

1. Remove leaves and woody ends, and discard tough or blemished stalks. Wash the rhubarb well under cold water, dry, and cut into 1-inch lengths.
2. Pack loosely and freeze. Or, mix 1 cup of sugar to each 4 cups of rhubarb pieces, pack, and freeze.

Strawberries: Dry-Pack

Prepare, pack, and freeze strawberries, as described for Raspberries.

Strawberries: Syrup-Pack

1. Sort berries carefully, discarding any imperfect specimens. Hull the berries, and wash quickly in cold water or ice water.
2. Make a 40 percent syrup solution (see page 79).
3. Pack containers with berries, and fill to within ½ inch of the rim with syrup. Seal and freeze.

10
Freezing Cooked Foods: Recipes

You can freeze almost any cooked food and expect it to come out well when thawed, provided you wrap it carefully and provided you use it within a reasonable length of time. In general, the taste and texture of cooked frozen meats and vegetables do not last as long as uncooked frozen foods.

Fully cooked leftover vegetables, such as baked beans and candied sweet potatoes, will keep for four to six months protected by the sauces that cover them. Plain, unsauced vegetables lose their flavor rapidly and should be stored for no more than one week. If you have a lot of leftover vegetables, cover with a cream sauce and plan to use within a month or two.

Stews and combination dishes can be stored for up to six months without loss of flavor. But do not freeze the stew vegetables. Cook fresh vegetables and add these to the stew when it is reheated for serving.

Baked goods keep well, especially breads, pie crusts, coffee cakes, and plain cakes.

Recipes for some foods that can be cooked and frozen are included at the end of this chapter. However, here is a quick guideline for the most commonly used foods frozen by this method.

Biscuits: These can be prepared and baked to a light brown, then cooled, packaged, sealed, and frozen. Don't forget to label.

Fruit and Nut Breads: Individually, nuts and fruits lose some of their texture during freezing, but fruit breads take the freezing process very well. Prepare and bake as usual, cool, package, and freeze.

Muffins: Bake to a light brown, cool, wrap, and freeze. Thaw and then bake at 275°F. before serving.

Waffles: Cook, cool, wrap very closely, and freeze. Heat before serving.

Bread and Rolls: Bake until just golden. Cool, wrap very closely, and freeze. To serve, thaw and brown in a 375°F oven for 10 minutes, and serve hot. Bread slices may be toasted without thawing.

Brown-and-Serve Rolls: Bake the rolls 20 minutes at 275°F. Cool, wrap well, and freeze. Thaw and bake at 375°F until brown. Serve hot.

Rolls, Unbaked: Make and shape the rolls. Wrap and freeze uncooked on baking sheets. Thaw and bake as instructed in the recipe.

Pizza Dough: Prepare dough; add sauce. Freeze uncooked and well-wrapped in freezer film. Thaw, proceed with recipe.

Cakes: Layer cakes, loaf cakes, cupcakes, angel cakes, chiffon cakes, and sponge cakes freeze with good results. Bake completely, and cool thoroughly. Wrap very carefully to exclude any air. Freeze. The cakes will require only a short period of defrosting before they are ready to serve. If a cake is to be iced, ice it while still frozen—it's easier!

Cookies, Baked: Cookies lose their crispness, but the flavor remains good after freezing. Bake, wrap carefully in freezer film, and draw the air from the wrapper. Seal, overwrap, and freeze. Thaw, and before serving, crisp briefly in a 275°F oven.

Cookies, Unbaked: Bar, or refrigerator, cookies are usually rolled in long rolls. They freeze well and retain their flavor as long as they are well wrapped. Thaw, cut into rounds, and finish baking. Or serve unbaked if the recipe calls for no cooking.

Doughnuts: Make dough; fry doughnuts. Do not sugar them. Wrap in freezer foil or polyethylene freezer bag. Overwrap and freeze. Thaw, warm in a 275°F oven; cool slightly, coat with sugar, and serve.

Gravy (not floured): Chill in the refrigerator, remove the fat that rises to the surface. Wrap loosely in a plastic bag, overwrap, and freeze. Be sure to label it. Beef gravy makes a good sauce for any meat; so does pork gravy; chicken gravy makes a good sauce for all fowl; lamb works well only for lamb; veal makes a good sauce for beef, chicken, or other fowl.

Pie Dough: Make dough, roll out, and cut into flat circles, large enough to fill your pie tins. Separate circles with thick freezer film or freezer paper; overwrap and freeze. Remove pie circles one at a time for use. Thaw, place in pie tin, proceed with recipe. Or roll out dough for single-crust pies, fit into aluminum pie plates, and freeze raw in the plates.

Pies: Almost all pies can be frozen, cooked or uncooked. Make fillings a little thicker than usual. Freeze uncooked cream pies and pies with sticky surfaces before wrapping in a fast-freezer compartment, or on the refrigerated surface where the freezing coils are situated. Then wrap the pies very closely with freezer film, overwrap, and store in the freezer. Serve cooked cream pies while still slightly frozen. Warm cooked two-crust pies to crisp the crusts before serving.

Salads: Salad greens do not freeze well—they don't even keep well in the refrigerator once mixed with dressing. Salads made of cottage cheese, whipped cream, mayonnaise, or gelatin with fruit or vegetables can be frozen if they would otherwise be wasted. They should be used as soon as possible and may "weep" when thawed.

Sandwiches: Chicken, meat, peanut butter, egg-yolk mixtures, fish, and jam sandwiches freeze well. Use within a few weeks.

Soups: Soups freeze well, including pea soup, bean soup, fish soups, vegetable soups, chicken, and other meat soups. If you have a large quantity to freeze, boil it down to one-half or one-third before freezing. To use later, thin to taste, with water or milk, after thawing. Pour soups to be frozen into the kettle they will be heated in at thawing: first line the kettle with freezer film. Freeze the soup in the kettle, then lift out the frozen soup in its wrapper, overwrap, seal, and store in the freezer. When it is time to heat the soup, it will fit into the kettle and will be quick to thaw over heat.

SMALL FREEZER CAN BE A GOURMET LARDER: If freezer space is limited, use it to hold homemade convenience foods, such as stocks, sauces, stews, casseroles, cakes and luxury meats and vegetables bought at bargain prices.

The Gourmet's Larder

Even if you have only a small freezer, you can use it to help with show-off cooking.

With just a few Oriental supplies and condiments—raw shrimp, minced or chopped pork in cup batches, egg-roll wrappers (sold by Oriental supply mail order houses and specialty food shops), frozen fresh ginger, green onions in strips or minced—you can use odds and ends of meats and vegetables in the refrigerator to throw together a delicious wok-cooked dish for two or more people.

With beef or chicken stocks in the freezer, you can create a Cordon Bleu casserole in hours less than it normally takes.

With pie shells, cakes, and other basic pastries on hand, you can create an aura of home cooking no matter who drops in at what hour, even if you've been slaving over a hot typewriter all day.

Below are recipes intended to show the range of foods you can cook and freeze.

Jams:

You can also make jam from berries by this recipe.

Frozen Peach Jam

1 qt peeled, pitted, chopped ripe peaches	1 (2-oz) package fruit pectin
½ cup strained lemon juice	1 cup Karo light corn syrup
	4½ cups sugar

1. In a glass bowl, crush chopped peaches until juices flow freely. Measure out 3¼ cups.
2. Stir the lemon juice into the peaches, and sift in the pectin. Stir vigorously. Set aside for 30 minutes.
3. Stir in corn syrup, and add sugar. Mix well. Stir over low heat just long enough to dissolve sugar crystals, but do not let the temperature of the mixture go above 100°F.
4. Ladel into pint or half-pint containers, leaving ½-inch head room. Cap, and freeze. Makes 7 half-pint jars.

Seasonings:

On pages 73–74 is a recipe for freezing herbs. You can also freeze combinations of fresh herbs in handy lots: here is my recipe for "bouquet garni," the herb combination used so often in French casseroles and gourmet dishes.

Bouquet Garni

Make a dozen, and store together in a plastic bag. This recipe makes one.

2 medium sprigs fresh parsley	1 bay leaf
	1 sprig fresh thyme

1. Tie parsley and thyme into a cheesecloth

bag, and blanch in boiling water for 30 seconds.

2. Dry well on paper towel, wrap, with bay leaf, into a small square of cheesecloth. Overwrap in plastic film, seal, and freeze.

Appetizers:

You can successfully freeze many appetizers —from Paté Maison, that delicious liver loaf offered by French restaurants, to Shrimp Toast, a favorite with Chinese meals.

Brandied Cheese Spread

4 Tbs butter	¼ cup brandy or
16 oz cream cheese	cognac
16 oz blue cheese	

1. At low speed, beat the butter and cheeses together until they are soft and completely blended. Beat in the brandy.
2. Pack into freezer-film lined half-pint containers, cover, and freeze. When frozen, remove the containers, overwrap, and store in the freezer.
   Thaw 4 hours before using. Stored in the refrigerator, the spread will be good for 2 or 3 months.
   Makes 8 half-pints.

Cheese Puffs

¼ lb sharp cheddar cheese, grated	½ tsp salt
	½ tsp paprika
¼ cup butter	1 small bottle of
½ cup flour, all purpose	small, stuffed olives

1. In a small bowl with the beater at low speed, beat the grated cheese into the butter. Add the flour, salt, and paprika, and mix at low speed. Gather the dough into a ball, and wrap it in wax paper. Store in the refrigerator overnight.
2. Warm for ½ hour, pinch off bits of the mix-

ture by the teaspoonful, flatten with your fingers to make a round pat, and wrap around the olives, which have been wiped dry. Gather the dough gently, leaving each end open, and roll between your palms to seal the sides of the dough.

3. Freeze, sealed in plastic freezer bags. Use within 6 months.
4. To serve, bake, still frozen, at 400°F for 15 minutes, or until golden brown. Serve at once.
   Makes about 30 balls.

Paté Maison

1 lb dark chicken meat, raw, bone in	1 small onion, peeled, stuck with 6 whole cloves
1 lb pork shoulder	
1¾ tsp salt	2 cups cold water
½ tsp black pepper	¾ lb chicken liver
1 bay leaf	1 cup chicken fat
1 tsp dried thyme	3 small cloves garlic, peeled and crushed
⅛ tsp allspice	
1 tsp savory	
½ bunch parsley, minced fine	

1. In a large kettle, place the chicken, pork, salt, pepper, bay leaf, thyme, allspice, savory, onion, and water. Cover and bring to a boil over medium heat. Simmer for 2 hours. Do not add more water.
2. Remove meat from the broth and reserve liquid. Remove the bones, chop all the meat finely.
3. Place the chicken livers in the cooking liquid, and simmer for 10 minutes. Remove and chop coarsely.
4. Discard bay leaf and onion. Add chicken fat to remaining cooking liquid, and boil rapidly for 5 minutes.
5. Put meat and liver through the blender at low speed, a cup at a time, each with some cooking liquid. Place the puréed meats in a large bowl, mix well with the garlic and parsley. Add salt and pepper to taste.
6. Line three 8-ounce (1 cup) molds with freezer film, and turn paté into these. Pat down flat, and smooth surfaces. Seal.

Freeze. Remove packages from molds, over-wrap, and store in freezer. Plan to use within a three-month period.

Thaw 3 or 4 hours before using. Store in refrigerator, and use thawed paté within 10 days.

Quiche

1 8-inch pie shell, baked and cooled	¾ cups Swiss cheese, finely grated
½ Tbs softened butter	½ tsp salt
8 slices bacon	⅛ tsp black pepper
3 whole eggs, plus 1 egg white	⅛ tsp nutmeg
1½ cups half-and-half	1 small onion, peeled, grated
	1 Tbs butter
	2 Tbs flour
1 Tbs butter	

1. Grease the cooled pie shell with the tablespoon of butter.
2. Sauté the bacon until crisp. Drain bacon on paper towel and crumble onto pie shell.
3. Beat the eggs until thick and lemon-colored. Beat in the half-and-half, cheese, salt, pepper, and nutmeg.
4. In a small saucepan, sauté the onion in 1 tablespoon butter until translucent. Mix in the flour, simmer 2 minutes, stirring. Beat slowly into the egg mixture. Turn the egg mixture into the pie shell, and dot with bits of butter.
5. Bake in a preheated 450°F oven for 15 minutes; turn heat down to 350°F, and bake another 15 minutes. Test with a silver knife. If the knife inserted in the center comes out clean, the quiche is done. If not, bake another 15 minutes, testing after each 5 minutes.
6. Cool and freeze unwrapped. When frozen, wrap in foil, overwrap in freezer paper, and store in freezer. Thaw and warm in 275°F oven for 15 minutes before serving. Plan to use within 6-month period.

Shrimp Toast

1 cup raw shrimp, shelled, deveined	¼ tsp ground ginger
	½ tsp salt
4 water chestnuts, minced	¼ tsp black pepper
	10 slices crustless bread
1 egg, slightly beaten	
1 Tbs dry sherry	
3 cups vegetable oil for deep frying	

1. Mince shrimp in blender at low speed, then blend in a medium bowl with water chestnuts, egg, sherry, ginger, salt, and pepper. Cut bread into even triangles, and spread shrimp paste *firmly* over them.
2. In a deep fryer, or a large kettle, heat the oil to 350°F, or until a bit of bread sizzles at once when dropped into the oil. Two or three at a time, lower the bread triangles into the oil, paste side down. When the edges brown, flip the triangles and brown on the other side. With a slotted spoon remove to paper towel, drain well, and cool.
3. Freeze, unwrapped, in fast-freezing compartment. When frozen, place in freezer bags, draw out the air, tie well, and store in freezer.
4. When ready to serve, remove the frozen triangles from the bag, drop into oil heated to 350°F for 1 minute. Or, simply warm in a preheated 350°F oven, and serve when crisped, about 10 minutes.

This recipe makes enough to serve 6 to 8 persons.

Please do use within 4-month period of freezing.

Soups and Stocks

Soups and stocks keep very well in the freezer. (See also Chapter 4, pages 40–41 and 42, for recipes for canning Chicken Stock and Beef Stock.) I can quantities of stock, as well as freezing a dozen or so cupfuls to have on hand to make small batches of sauces for meats and to use in braising vegetables. Frozen stock is good for 6 months.

Hearty winter soups can be made from many ingredients from the frozen food compartment or locker. Peas, spinach, okra, tomatoes, shrimp, beef, or chicken may be defrosted and cooked as you would any basic thick soup, especially when the single basic ingredient is blended, seasoned, and simmered.

Below is my favorite recipe for pea soup. Save, wrap closely, and freeze bones from roasts. Use lamb bones to make barley soup; beef bones, including steak and roast bones (but not bones of steaks that have been barbecued), to add to beef stock and vegetable soup. Freeze chicken parts (but use within three months) to collect enough to make chicken soup or chicken stock. Frozen bones can be stored 6 to 8 months without deteriorating.

SOUP USING INGREDIENTS FROM FREEZER: Here a rich tomato soup is garnished with bits of frozen onion and green pepper, and decorated with ornamental slices of cucumber added raw at the last moment.

Pea Soup with a Ham Bone

2 Tbs butter	1 ham bone, plus any meat attached to it
1 cup peeled, minced onion	
12 cups cold water	1 cup celery, finely chopped
2 cups (1 lb) green split peas, dried	
4 whole cloves	1 cup diced, scraped carrot
1 bay leaf	⅛ tsp savory, dried
	1 Tbs salt
	¼ tsp pepper

1. In a large soup kettle, melt the butter over low heat, and simmer the onion until translucent. Add water and all other ingredients, cover and bring to a boil. Reduce heat and simmer for 4 hours, or until peas have completely disintegrated. Stir occasionally as soup thickens, adding more water if it becomes very thick.
2. Remove ham bone, bay leaf, and cloves. Dice the ham from the bone, and return diced ham to the soup. Add salt and pepper to taste.

Makes 10 to 12 generous portions. Freeze leftover pea soup. It is good for 6 months.

Shrimp Bisque

Thaw and blend 1½ pounds of large cleaned shrimp. Cook in the top of a double boiler with 6 tablespoons of butter and 2 tablespoons of grated onion for 5 minutes. A little at a time blend the above with 3 cups of milk, added slowly. Remove and heat in the top of the double boiler, stirring in 1 cup of cream. Salt to taste, and add a pinch of nutmeg, 3 tablespoons of sherry, and garnish with 2 tablespoons of chopped chives.
Yields 5 cups.

Stews and Roasts

Roasts and turkey (when there's too much left over from Thanksgiving, for instance,) freeze very well. If possible, prepare the extra meat for the freezer while the meat is still lukewarm because at that point it holds a lot of moisture. Slice the meat ¼-inch thick and pack, separating individual portions with double thicknesses of freezer paper. Dribble over the meat any available pan dripping (remove the fat first), then seal and freeze. Before serving, defrost, and warm, covered with a very damp towel, in an oven at 350°F.

Frozen stews and casseroles are good for 6 months. Freeze stews without the vegetables because these lose their texture. Prepare fresh vegetables while the stew is defrosting—4 to 5 hours—and heat them in the stew before serving.

When I make the veal stew recipe below, I use half fresh, with all the vegetables, and freeze the balance without vegetables. Before serving the frozen portions, I thaw it 3 to 4 hours, heat it to just below boiling, and serve it over boiled rice.

Blanquette de Veau

This can also be made with the white meat of chicken.

2 lbs boned veal shoulder, cut in 2-inch pieces	1 tsp salt
	1 bay leaf
	¼ cup butter
1 qt boiling water	1 lb (15) small white onions, peeled
1 small onion, peeled, stuck with 5 whole cloves	
	½ lb small mushrooms, stemmed
5 scraped, quartered carrots	2 Tbs butter
⅛ tsp dried thyme	¼ cup all-purpose flour
½ cup dried celery	
4 peppercorns	2 egg yolks
	2 Tbs lemon juice
1 Tbs minced parsley	

1. In a large kettle, simmer the veal with the next 8 ingredients for 1 hour. Drain and reserve the stock; place the veal in an ovenproof casserole with the carrots and celery. Discard the onion, bay leaf, and peppercorns.
2. Melt ¼ cup butter in a medium skillet, and simmer the onions, covered, for 15 to 25 minutes, until completely cooked. With a slotted spoon, remove the cooked onions to the veal casserole. In the same skillet, sauté the mushrooms, uncovered, for 15 minutes, then add these to the casserole.
3. Melt 2 tablespoons of butter in the skillet over very low heat, stir in the flour and then stir in the reserved veal stock. Still stirring, simmer the stock until it thickens.
4. Beat the egg yolks with the lemon juice. Stir ¼ cup of hot stock into the yolks, then turn the yolks into the stock. Over very low heat, simmer, stirring, for 5 minutes. Pour over the veal. To serve fresh, garnish the casserole with minced parsley. (When reheating, do not boil. Add the parsley garnish before serving.)

Serves 6 to 8 portions.

SPRINGTIME STEW IN MIDWINTER: Two cups of frozen chicken stock are set out to thaw, together with one cup of frozen, cooked chicken, with frozen chopped onion, peas, and chopped green peppers from their frozen plastic bags. Thaw also a few small frozen tomatoes. Dice two potatoes and slice two carrots thin, simmering them in the unfrozen stock. When the carrots can be pierced easily with a fork, the chicken and other thawed ingredients are added and simmered. Add a pinch of thyme, a bay leaf, a pinch of ground clove, and a teaspoon of curry at the same time until the flavors have combined.

Freezing Stews:

The wise way of creating a wide variety of frozen stews that will taste fresh when served is a good cook's trick. Freeze beef and chicken stock by the cupful. Freeze cooked or uncooked chicken or meat, cut into stew-sized pieces, in the small quantities that you would ordinarily put in your family-sized stew.

When about to prepare the stew, defrost the meat and stock. While it is defrosting, cut into stew-sized pieces and cook whatever fresh vegetables you have chosen—carrots, potatoes, celery—anything you would add to a fresh-made stew. Undercook them slightly, so that when you put the defrosted meat, the unfrozen stock, and the vegetables in the stewpot to simmer together, the flavors will blend. Add seasonings at this time.

If you are using raw stew meat, thaw it and then sear it quickly over high heat. Add to the stock and cook thoroughly before the freshly cooked vegetables are added. When you have leftover cooked rice, barley, or other grains, these too can be frozen in small quantities to include later in a stew. They should be added at the same time as the cooked vegetables.

A nice touch, if you wish, is to add bite-sized pieces of raw vegetables such as tomato, water chestnut, cucumber, or parsley to the stew just before serving. A very wide variety of stews can be created in this way if you have kept on hand those small packets of cooked or uncooked ingredients that freeze well with no loss of freshness.

Salad Dressings:

Oil and vinegar dressing can be frozen. Pour it into a small plastic storage bag, set into a freezer container, freeze, then remove, and pack in a large freezer bag. It will stay fresh for 6 to 8 months. Below is my favorite salad dressing.

Oil and Vinegar Dressing

6 Tbs olive oil, or vegetable oil	¼ tsp granulated sugar
1½ Tbs vinegar	1 tsp salt
⅛ tsp dried mustard	⅛ tsp pepper

1. Put all ingredients into a blender, and mix at low speed.
   Makes about ¼ cup.
   Freeze as described above, and allow 1 hour for thawing before using.

Desserts:

Frozen desserts make it so easy to prepare a festive dinner that I keep many on hand. Below is my recipe for layer cake, one that freezes exceptionally well, keeps unfrosted, up to 6 months, and makes a super layer cake for impromptu birthday celebrations.

Layer Cake

3 cups sifted cake flour	2 cups granulated sugar
3 tsp baking powder	4 eggs, unbeaten
⅛ tsp salt	1 cup milk
1 cup shortening (butter or Crisco)	1 tsp vanilla extract

1. Preheat the oven to 375°F.
2. Measure the flour, baking powder, and salt into a sifter, set into a large bowl, and sift three times.
3. In a large bowl, with an electric beater, cream the shortening with the sugar until fluffy. One at a time, add the eggs, beating well after each addition. Add the sifted flour, alternately with the milk, in thirds, and beat smooth after each addition. Add the vanilla, and blend in.
4. Butter two 8-inch square, or round, cake tins. Pour the batter into the pans and bake 25 minutes, or until a straw inserted in the center of the cake comes out clean.
5. Cool on a cake rack, wrap in plastic freezer foil, overwrap in freezer paper, and freeze.
6. Allow ½ hour for defrosting before serving. Ice while frozen.
   Serves 10 to 12 persons.

Index